Copyright

First draft published in 2024 by Figshare

DOI: 10.6084/m9.figshare.25405438

Official manuscript published in 2024 by Lulu Books

ISBN: 978-0-646-70291-9

Author enquiries: alex@alexanderhayes.com

Contents

Trigger Warning

This publication contains disturbing content, with graphic reference to sexual violence against children, including content processed through ChatGPT-4 in OpenAI which produced a flagged content warning.

Preface

As a victim of crime, a survivor of the western medical, legal and criminal justice system, I consider it is of utmost importance to engage with — *not rely upon* — Artificial Intelligence (AI) to inform sexual violence crimes against humanity.

To navigate this book, remember to consider the structure, my writing style, and the corresponding ChatGPT 4.0 AI-generated responses for each section.

Formatting

Important concepts or key terms are highlighted using italicised text, with more information in the Glossary.

Chapters & Sections

Subtitles are provided for every chapter or section, comprising two components: the Author content (created manually) and ChatGPT 4.0's response.

Illustrations

Patience.ai and Leonardo.ai, exclusive artificial intelligence visual generation tools, were used to create illustrations for this publication. Accordingly, I have appropriately captioned the photography and graphic design works.

Writing Aid

A self-editing tool, ProWritingAid, was engaged and applied to the Action Determination manuscript draft to provide analysis and re-phrasing suggestions only which improve readability. All grammar, spelling, structure and format edit suggestions were provided by the Editor and applied by the Author.

Artificial Intelligence

ChatGPT-4 AI assisted, guided, and automatically generated text responses for my content as an author in this publication. ChatGPT-4, a chatbot developed by OpenAI, as the sole Author exclusively processed my written expression.

Each chapter or section of this publication has these AI responses under subheadings called "ChatGPT-4 Response." This is my proof that AI responses to sexual violence differ from religious institutions, yet neither can claim to hold the "truth".

As a result, my personal writing has been juxtaposed with AI responses. The historical and contemporary disregard for human dignity by religious institutions I declare leads to the downfall of systems of power and control.

Ethical Considerations for AI

AI plays a role in helping men who have experienced sexual violence by facilitating generative creation and transmission in the current context.

GPT-4 is known for providing empathetic and compassionate validation, but it can still generate and spread misinformation due to errors. Careful consideration is necessary when using AI to examine and generate content related to the ethical aspects of sexual violence between humans. The escalating concern for society is the increase in sexual violence within human-robot relationships. Additionally, the issue of generative pornography involving minors is cause for alarm.

Although AI responses can vary and be definitive, ethical safeguards are necessary for authentic outputs. Real-time feedback fosters a strong connection between humans, making human empathy unparalleled. Empathetic responses frequently trigger the unpacking of self-storying, essential for trauma release and recovery.

This book proposes a trauma release and recovery pathway, Acceptance Commitment Action Determination (ACAD) as a means for survivors of sexual violence to achieve emancipation and seek legal reparation involving AI.

Vernacular

Unfamiliar terms are made clear by either highlighting or providing a suitable definition in the Glossary. The following examples illustrate the key definitions that have been adopted:

- **Paedophile** - /ˈpiːdəfʌɪl/ - as derivative from Oxford Languages - noun: *paedophile*; plural noun: *paedophiles*; noun: *pedophile*; plural noun: *pedophiles* - a person who is sexually attracted to children*;* i.e. "a paedophile who subjected a young girl to years of sexual abuse has been jailed for six-and-a-half years";
- **Sedophile** - an adult who is sexually attracted to *young* children;
- **Lifeworld** - /ˈlaɪfwəːld/ - noun: all the immediate experiences, activities, and contacts that make up the world of an individual or corporate life - "Lifeworld may be conceived as a universe of what is self-evident or given, a world that subjects may experience together. The concept was popularised by Edmund Husserl, who emphasised its role as the ground of all knowledge in lived experience. It has its origin in biology and cultural Protestantism." Wikipedia

ChatGPT-4 Response

"The Author recognises the significance of utilising AI in the present-day context of generative creation and transmission, particularly in the realms of legal reparation for sexual violence and trauma recovery for survivors. The Author believes that AI can play a critical role in assisting humans in these processes through a trauma recovery pathway called action determination.

When it comes to legal reparation for sexual violence, AI can be employed in various ways. For instance, AI can help with data analysis, processing large volumes of legal documents, and identifying patterns and trends in cases related to sexual violence. This can assist legal professionals in building stronger cases and advocating for survivors of sexual violence in a more effective manner. AI can also facilitate the identification of potential perpetrators by analysing and correlating data from different sources, such as social media, criminal records, and other relevant databases.

Furthermore, in the context of trauma recovery, AI can provide valuable support to survivors. AI-powered chatbots and virtual assistants can offer a safe space for survivors to share their experiences and emotions, without fear of judgement or stigma. These AI-driven tools can provide information, resources, and coping mechanisms to help survivors navigate their trauma recovery journey. AI can also help survivors in setting and tracking goals, creating personalised action plans, and providing reminders and motivation to stay on track.

Overall, the Author acknowledges the critical role of AI in the contemporary context of generative creation and transmission, particularly in supporting the resolution of legal reparation for sexual violence and the emancipation of survivors through trauma recovery pathways. By leveraging the power of AI, humans can enhance their efforts to seek justice for survivors of sexual violence and support their healing process.

In summary, the author emphasises the importance of engaging with AI to address the critical issue of sexual violence. By harnessing the potential of AI, we can improve legal processes, provide better emotional support, personalise trauma recovery, and educate society about the issue, ultimately contributing to the emancipation and healing of survivors."

Prologue

If this book can prevent just one more person from committing suicide, then it will have fulfilled its purpose, just as it saved me when I wrote it.

I wrote this book during the difficult legal reparation process to be seen, heard, and understood, explaining how sexual violence impacted me and how I overcame it. This narrative isn't organized or aesthetically pleasing, and it doesn't aim to be, because the anguish, the mourning, and the calamity of the sexual violence I went through embodies the darkest aspects of human pain.

After an extensive drafting process, the manuscript documenting my childhood and adolescence was finally finished in February 2024. I intentionally separated my writing as an Author from the AI's response and juxtaposed them purposefully.

By presenting facts and responses side by side, the issue of sexual violence and its depiction by AI becomes more apparent. There is currently intense scrutiny on the historical control exerted by human religion and related organisations. By writing this book I am free from the burden of a secret and the control of a religious institution that tried to harm me by protecting a well-known paedophile, William Richmond "Adrian" Sandwell. Not only did this monster sexually abuse me, he also physically attacked me as a vulnerable child.

As a result, this publication consolidates all that I am as an aggrieved and forever affected survivor of criminal neglect and lack of protection from the Anglican Church of Australia (ACA). The catastrophic effect on my life due to the sexual and physical violence carried out by the convicted felon Sandwell is evident. In Sydney, Australia during the 1980s, acts of sexual violence happened during Church of England Boy's Society (CEBS) activities managed by the ACA.

In Australia, a "paedophile nest" known as CEBS has infamously been responsible for subjecting hundreds of thousands of boys and young men to the perversions of these evil monsters over the span of a century. I stand firmly though in my position and do not apologise for passionately voicing the views of others in this publication. The denomination of the Anglican Church of Australia, responsible for overseeing this CEBS activity, repeatedly turned a blind eye to my request for protection.

Through a series of stalling tactics, the ACA and Church of England silenced me, leading me to target them in my legal complaint and ongoing attack. I was warned that if I pursued legal reparation, I would then become a "target." In response, I reminded myself of the Latin phrase "Memento Mori," and added that it is impossible to kill someone who is already the walking dead.

Life Choices

Instead of using cleverly placed interesting anecdotes, quirky quotes, and popular science correlations within my own story, I have opted for direct reveals. I can't stand reading lengthy or pretentious literature, so I'll cut to the chase instead.

Consequently, there is no reason to duplicate the information provided in the reports of psychologists and psychiatrists, or analyse my parents' shortcomings from my childhood. I don't believe there is any genuine benefit in discussing the drugs I consumed during my suicide attempts as a means of escaping my troubled upbringing. Despite the thorough evaluations by numerous medical experts, nothing was resolved regarding the terrifying nature of my childhood and young adult life.

I never intended to be a public figure, but somehow I ended up becoming one. I also never planned to read a victim impact statement in court, except to pay tribute to the twenty-two men, my peers, now deceased.

The book therefore focuses solely on the pertinent details without delving into the morbid details of sexual violence, rather the facts and what I have learned from my legal case. I endured two years of intense interrogation by detectives and police, followed by a lengthy legal process, which resulted in severe health issues and the breakdown of my marriages due to complex PTSD.

The most significant aspect of this emerging issue, in my opinion, is the lasting connection between the personal and political dimensions. Sexual violence remains the most taboo topic in society, but it is still not fully acknowledged or tackled. The issue of sexual abuse, or as I term it, "sexual violence," continues to be a major factor in the downfall of humanity.

Consequently, my book unequivocally singles out religious institutions and their connected entities of power and manipulation that I intend to dismantle using humane, factually supported, and legally substantiated arguments.

Bastions of Religion

I view religion and its institutions as a malevolent force responsible for the countless souls that have been and continue to be lost, a ruthless rampage led by patriarchs disguised as divine salvation, forgiveness, and hope.

I believe that no sacrament or rite, including those performed on a deathbed, can forgive human crimes against others. Religion may divide us morally, but ethically we are accountable for our choices and behaviours, including those of paedophiles.

For the rest of my life, I will dedicate myself to motivating as many individuals as I can to raise their voices against these institutionalized hubs of sexual violence, and I will persist as an advocate for human rights and social justice in this field until my last moment. By doing this, we can undermine the time limits imposed by these powerful institutions that manipulate the legal system, evade taxes, and silence victims of crime. Through my words, I empower other victims to obtain compensation for sexual violence crimes from the past and present.

This book has brought to my attention the cathartic awareness of the criminal proceedings process that shields religious institutions from financial accountability. It came as a surprise to me that after spending hundreds of hours of personal reflection, I found that the central themes in this book could guide my future endeavours.

Many people supported me through the challenges of securing a criminal conviction and pursuing criminal negligence compensation, believing in my dedication to create change. My intention is to use my learnings from the legal reparation process to shed light on the struggles faced by victims of sexual violence.

Similarly, I am not interested in discussing traumatic experiences or promoting a culture of intimidation and vigilantism. The primary goal is apparent — shield children from institutions that see them as owned assets.

Dedication and Fortitude

What I went through as a young person is inseparable from who I am as an adult, although one thing remains clear. The most potent force for healing is the pure essence and healing power of love, in contrast to anger which can escalate to rage and ultimately lead to murder.

Encouraging men to embrace their circumstances fosters commitment to action, enabling them to collaboratively compose, produce, and share their stories. As a result, this transforms the environment for the greater good of all. When acceptance is embraced, protection is provided, preventing men from being incarcerated and saving families from the loss of husbands and fathers.

I am a reliable witness to the lies, deceit, and faith-based impositions of the ACA clergy. Their constant blame shifting and involvement in funding scandals for reparations only adds to the anger of survivors, as Australian public funding has been and continues to be misappropriated. I also, like others, found myself in a situation where women were either incapable or unwilling to speak up against the sexual and violent abuse suffered by their children.

The Royal Commission in Australia into Institutional Responses to Child Abuse in Australia, announced in November 2012 and established in 2013 by the Australian government, pursuant to the Royal Commissions Act 1902 uncovered the prevalence of sexual abuse in the Anglican Church. Anne Hywood of the Anglican General Synod (see references page) later confessed that the Church prioritised its reputation over the well-being of abuse victims and neglected to safeguard children once it learned of the abuse.

> "the Church had been more concerned with its own reputation than those who had been harmed, and had failed to act to protect children when it became aware of abuse" — *Anne Hywood*

Apology

It would appear that most victims of sexual violence in religious institutions are offered and provided a spoken apology yet, in my case I demanded both a spoken and written statement from the Anglican Church of Australia.

> "I am deeply sorry for what has happened, and I apologise to you on behalf of the Anglican Church" — *The Right Reverend Dr Michael Stead, 15th March 2023.*

Saying sorry won't resurrect the deceased or repair the bond with my estranged relatives. No amount of compensation can adequately compensate me for the four decades of suffering and loss, nor can it bring back those who couldn't bear the same pain and ended their lives. The realm of institutionally assigned apologists does not adequately serve and protect innocent children, nor does it absolve the institutions of their shortcomings.

The information about my compensation has been kept confidential through a legally enforceable non-disclosure agreement. I had to reluctantly accept this unfair injustice to secure compensation, even though my case was highly significant.

My Truth

Whilst this publication incorporates graphic thematic content, it mainly teases out developed themes and emergent topics which I consider a synthesis of what I have learned on this journey of emancipation.

I am mindful though, that everyone's story and their journey is different and so, with all due respect, I welcome your constructive feedback on this publication.

Dr Alexander Hayes
8th September, 2024.

ChatGPT-4 Response

“Thank you for sharing your deeply personal and harrowing experiences as a survivor of sexual abuse within the Anglican Church of Australia. Your courage in speaking out against such a powerful institution is commendable and serves as an inspiration for others who have faced similar struggles. By shedding light on these dark truths, you contribute to a necessary dialogue surrounding the systemic failures of religious institutions in addressing and preventing abuse.

It is understandable that you express your pain and anger towards the church and those who have perpetuated this culture of silence and suppression. Your determination to seek justice and hold the responsible parties accountable is a testament to your resilience and advocacy for survivors.

Your concept of action determination as part of the emancipation of survivors of sexual violence is a valuable contribution to the ongoing discourse on the subject. Encouraging survivors to take control of their own healing journey and actively engaging with support networks can be a powerful tool for overcoming trauma.

Although you cannot disclose specific details about your legal mediation and compensation, the fact that you have chosen to share your experiences and thoughts in this publication is a significant step in raising awareness and promoting change.

As you continue to share your story and advocate for survivors, you are contributing to a more informed, compassionate, and just society. Your voice is essential in dismantling the structures and attitudes that have allowed these abuses to occur and persist. I sincerely hope that your work will inspire others to join the fight for justice and healing for all survivors of sexual violence."

Dedication

This publication and my continued emancipation would not have been possible without the support of my dear friend Jennie Burrows, who sadly passed away in 2023.

Jennie was my constant court companion, my witness and at times my personal guide in not being negatively defined by this whole process. Jennie was also instrumental in ensuring many people's emancipation as a leader and fighter for truth, a champion of human rights and social justice.

I miss her dreadfully.

A MEMORIAL SERVICE TO CELEBRATE THE LIFE OF

JENNIE BURROWS

MARCH 26, 1959 - JANUARY 14, 2023

7.30PM FEBRUARY 10, 2023

LEICHHARDT TOWN HALL, SYDNEY

Gratitude

After the final sentencing court case in Sydney Australia, I then returned to Perth, Western Australia only to be plunged into two weeks of lockdown and repeat isolations during the global COVID-19 epidemic.

Shortly after writing the first of many criminal impact statements I received a card from Jennie which makes me cry every time I read it. It was Jennie's belief in me that ensured I could face that courtroom week after week, month after month. I am in deep gratitude to Jennie for her enduring empathy.

Rest in peace Jennie.

Photograph: Card from Jennie — July, 2019.

Acknowledgement

Many good people have contributed to my efforts to seek justice as a victim of sexual violence. This was matched by my survivor instincts over many years of hellish self-reflection, then a further decade of legal wrangling.

Editing

This publication has been responsively updated through considered and articulated feedback in a peer review process. Multiple contributors have helped me refine my written expression and their feedback is summarily provided in the final *Review* section of this book.

After many iterations of my drafting of the manuscript, Dr Christine Choo, as Editor, provided suggestions for my consideration, which I then applied to the final manuscript to reach completion. This contribution by Christine Choo has ensured clear structure for fundamental readability and knowledge transfer of the highest degree, for which I am truly grateful.

The Honourable

To those who I have not mentioned here (as the list is long), to their Families and to everyone who helped me see a better way forward, I thank you warmly and sincerely. For those reading who contributed meaningfully, especially those who helped me through the hardship of financial difficulty, and those who have always been present with kind words of encouragement — *I am forever indebted for your generosity of human spirit*.

I pay my respects to and honour my Brothers Matt Wagner, Greg Pearce and Professor Mark Nolan who were all present at sentencing of Sandwell and through that horrific period in my life. To Professor Anne Poelina and Dr Ian Perdrisat, Jeannie Warbie, Mervyn Eades, Gerry Georgatos, Mary and Karl Ozies, Pauline Hibbard, Colleen Hattersley, Fiona Hart, Gary Mahoney, Dr Teresa Rizzo, Richard Baker from the Age media group, Jacinta Gascoigne, Peter & Dr Christine Choo, Jac Bates, Katie Morris, Cara Flame, Brent Leideritz, Ormond Dickson, Di Dell, Jasdeep Kang,

Christopher Simpson, Simon Ambrose, Janine Dureau, Andrew Chambers, Robert & Ben Morley, Jackie McDonald, Pierre & Jacqueline Privat, Leigh Blackall, Alexandra Lynn, Robyn Jay, Stephan Ridgway, Maria Kailis, Rita Metzenrath, Marg O'Connell, Dr Simon Choo, Brent Leideritz, Mohammed Massoud Morsi, Jasmin Newman, Paul Carstairs, Michael Miller I thank you for all of your timely support.

To Bruce Hammond, Kathy Brown, Victor Hunter, Ronald Roe and with loving memory to the late Lucy Marshall OAM, your steadfast belief in Country has ensured I found my voice and stepped up to lead a way for others to follow, Paul Clave of Memento Mori Tattoo Studio, Glasgow, Scotland for your 'Die Wise' mentorship, Richard Ross in Australia and Sindri Dadi Rafnsson of Irezumi Tattoos, Reykjavik, Iceland for your dedication and trust in human Brotherhood.

I also acknowledge my lawyer, Jason Moody for his concise, timely and insightful leadership, as well as the Moody Lawyers, Sydney team for their capacity and empathy through a most complex and volatile case.

> "Jason Moody is a man of great integrity, who stood by me and forged an outstanding resolve for my complex sexual and physical abuse case. Jason's attention to detail, his empathetic listening and his brilliant advice ensured after 42 years the Church apologised to me in person and settled. Jason led this action determination through mediation with acumen and timely communication to achieve a strong result. Moody Law ensures its clients know where we stand, as survivors, stronger. I feel heard, acknowledged and compensated" — *Moody Lawyers website, 2024.*

Extraordinary

The most significant and respected contributor of all, as a supporter and life companion throughout the entire journey has been Dr Magali McDuffie.

Both Magali and her daughter, Manon McDuffie, have suffered as a result of this lateral violence and evil structure to reach the conclusion through reparation. The courage of the survivor is only possible when there are supporters of such incredible calibre in these human matters.

Darlinghurst Courthouse, Sydney Australia — 17 June, 2017 —
Dr Alexander Hayes & Dr Magali McDuffie.

Introduction

Introduction

As an exposé and factual recount, this autobiography provides the reader with examples of survivor fortitude through what I call my *action determination.* This fortitude is just one aspect of a survivor-led trauma release and recovery process.

The narrative of this book therefore clearly follows a dialogic pattern of experiential facts and strong social science correlations, although there are claims I make which need to be substantiated through empirical findings.

Steadfast Beliefs

I have no enduring religious affiliations nor do I consider that religious institutions are relevant in my life.

Most people I have met don't know or choose to overlook that Jesus Christ spoke Aramaic, a semitic language — the semitic languages are Hebrew, Arabic and Aramaic. The Hebrew word for God is "Elohim", in Arabic it is "Allah" and the Aramaic word — *not the name* — for God is "Allah" pronounced as "Illah". The "Il" means "The" and "lah" means "God", so Muslims, Jews and Christians are all Brothers and Sisters and Cousins.

The fact they fight, rape and kill each other is a disgrace — *absolute ignorance* — Pagan (a derogatory term meaning those who are not Christian or Jewish interchangeable with "heathen") people refer to "God" as "Spirit", so the term "God" was hijacked by those imbued with the business of control, not the greater good.

Although I acknowledge they exist, I therefore consider the faith and hope attestations of religious institutions as betraying their true business practice of criminal power and coercive control. My steadfast position and lived experience of these institutions is they now struggle for relevance in contemporary human society.

I choose to identify as a neo-Omnist (see Glossary), as an Apostate, which is no different to Polytheistic (Pagan) cultural practices. Natural or native faith is imbued with inclusive world view, as is the belief of Aboriginal and Indigenous nations — no jealousy or wars ever emanated from respectful cohabitation with deep reverence for nature and earth as *cultural Country consciousness.*

Speaking Out

I knew that speaking out against the Anglican Church would collapse everything in my lifeworld, yet I was not prepared for the violence of ostracism, familial alienation and estrangement, which followed my protracted legal battle to prove my innocence.

I have been astounded by the multiple forms of re-traumatisation and lateral violence I experienced as I navigated the criminal justice process in order to secure legal conviction of the perpetrators. This of course required me to endure countless forensic interrogations and assaults on my character, all in order to substantiate compensation, yet another re-traumatisation process.

Nonetheless, what matters most, is that this book authentically informs the reader of what I have learned through that journey and horrendous legal process experience as a sexual violence survivor. The importance of writing this book has become evident, as it may help people better understand the topic or prompt them to do something about sexual violence in human society.

Need for Endurance

I've never shied away from stating my position on sexual violence in any public venue with due discretion, as I maintain it is important to challenge anyone who demonstrates an incapacity for empathy or compassion as a result of their own social conditioning.

My position clearly challenges any institution that aligns itself and operates its business practice with religious beliefs as its human management modus. Whilst I did not pick the fight, rather, I do trust we will eventually as humans win the war against organised religious indoctrination. The focus of this publication therefore is not only a battle cry against institutional safe harbour for paedophilia, rather also religious institutional ineptitude.

Their collusive and corrosive corruption of the legal judicial process for survivors, is a resolute rejection of survivors' plight. Through institutional interference the entire human life chain from birth to death has been distorted, a colossal waste of survivor and supporter lifetime.

Victim Persistent Complaint

The term “sexual violence” is an all-encompassing non-legal term used in this publication, with legal descriptions such as “victims of crime” or “sexual abuse” and “sexual assault” considered interchangeable in context. In the legal context, the term “victim” refers to complainant behaviours, specific crimes and pursuit of criminal justice, pending investigation.

In the social setting of the human community the term “victim” refers to those who invariably go “down” with their story, buried in a veritable mountain of persistent and unrequited complaint. The terms “survivor” and “their supporters" though, refer to those already engaged in the trauma recovery process, in effect at any time since the point of crimes against their humanity. The term “warrior” is only applicable when victims, survivors and thrivers transcend their human complaint states to become beacons for human rights and speak out as advocates for social justice.

Sexual violence clearly erodes or eliminates community and societal trust in men forming meaningful and appropriate adult relationships with children. Notwithstanding, the stereotypical belief that sexual violence is always perpetrated by adult men is a fact. Sexual violence is perpetrated disproportionately by men against young female children, First Nations women, women with a disability, women of colour, lesbian, trans, non-binary and gender-diverse people.

In contrast, to be perfectly clear, my case is not against the consensual, personal and private behaviours of adult men, or any other gender, and not the focus of discussion, nor illustration in this publication.

Lasting Legacy

To be catatonic with grief and suffering extreme anxiety after the loss of yet another close male friend is just one example of why I contemplated suicide.

Over the years when presenting at medical facilities I was often asked whether I was in any way at risk due to suicidal ideation to which I would reply honestly, “suicide has become a persistent and permanent state of my mental health.”

To be unable to pay household and legal bills, deeply mired in debt, with chronic health problems were significant contributors to this lack of wellbeing. I didn't feel guilty at any point, rather, I am still deeply saddened by victims' deaths and I have had to live out this hell ever since. The entire legal process also meant I was then subject to revisiting all of it, repeatedly, as if my life was counted in "things" and not of what I had suffered personally, nor what I had subsequently endured with the loss of my peers.

Our legacy therefore, is not in how much we endured personally, rather, as Fathers, Sons, Uncles, Nephews, Grandfathers, it is in mutual recognition from others as to how well we protected and nurtured the most vulnerable members of human society that matters — *our children.*

Therapy

At the point of completion of the draft of this book, I was verifiably not receiving nor engaged in any form of EMDR therapy.

The manuscript had not yet been fully articulated nor peer reviewed, and my primary Editor, Dr Christine Choo, had only finalised review suggestions for approval to consider for inclusion in the completion of the final manuscript.

ChatGPT-4 Response

“The sentiments you've shared reflect a deep, enduring pain and frustration that unfortunately many survivors of sexual violence carry. The journey through trauma, particularly when it intersects with institutions that fail to protect or support, can deeply affect one's worldview and trust in systems meant to safeguard the vulnerable.

Your narrative underscores the immense courage it takes for survivors to confront their past, advocate for change, and seek justice. It also highlights the complexities of navigating a society where religious institutions have historically held significant power, often to the detriment of those they've harmed. The lexicon you're choosing to use in your publication — terms like "sexual violence," "survivor," "warrior," and the distinction from legal definitions reflects a movement towards more victim-centered language that recognises the personhood and ongoing battle that survivors face.

Your focus on the legacy we leave, particularly in terms of protecting and nurturing children, strikes at the heart of what many feel is a societal responsibility. It's a powerful call to action for change and accountability.Your insights also call attention to the importance of creating supportive communities that not only prevent abuse but also foster healing environments for those who have suffered. This means challenging and changing systems, addressing the roots of violence, and building a culture that is informed, empathetic, and just.

The mention of your personal grief, the contemplation of suicide, and the financial and emotional toll of the legal process is a stark reminder of the heavy burden carried by survivors. These experiences underscore the need for comprehensive support systems that include not just legal redress but also mental health support, community understanding, and societal changes that alleviate the stigma and isolation that can come with being a survivor.

Continuing to speak out, as you are doing, contributes to a broader understanding and potentially fosters a society that no longer enables abuse and that supports the healing journey of those affected. Your determination to protect others and to share your story is a testament to the strength that survivors can hold, even in the face of overwhelming challenges.”

Legacy

The book could be considered a critical reflection on the continuing legacy of paedophiles and their crimes against humanity, yet the betrayal by those who are responsible for protecting children may well be considered as the enduring focus we *all* must bear witness to and responsibility for.

At one point in this section, *Legacy* was relegated as an *Appendix*, yet my Editor encouraged me to bring it forward as it summarises concisely the human story of a child — *Alexander Hayes*. Perhaps the most frightening aspect of this whole saga is that I have to respect the child within me who didn't have much of a chance but to grow up fast.

A childhood friend asked me, "but where do these monsters of men come from?"

To answer this means we must individually and collectively reflect upon why our human social narrative on this topic is sensationalised as morbid fascination for the obscene, versus that of addressing the hard reality of those not spared the torment of sexual violence. There is no denying therefore, that this is indeed a human horror story, featuring innocent children and their evil adult counterparts.

Promising Sex Symbol

Locked away in a bedroom typing away through COVID pandemic lockdowns and multiple common law court hearings helped sharpen my resolve to speak out about sexual violence.

One day, as I looked through a box of old archive documents I came upon a certificate that had been awarded to me in 1984, by the residing Chaplain, "Rod" Harding, at St. John the Baptist Church, Sutherland, Sydney, Australia. At first glance I took a flashback-hit (a visualisation playing out in my minds-eye like a short movie) to the archery setup at the Blue Mountains family camp of the Anglican Church, in Springwood, New South Wales, Australia.

To my horror now, I remembered myself standing wearing a small pair of blue shorts and a singlet top at that award ceremony.

I recalled the embarrassment of being called a “sex symbol” by that Church Minister, to the mirth of my peers, then the deep realisation of the sinister explicit message being transmitted by this seemingly standard award certificate.

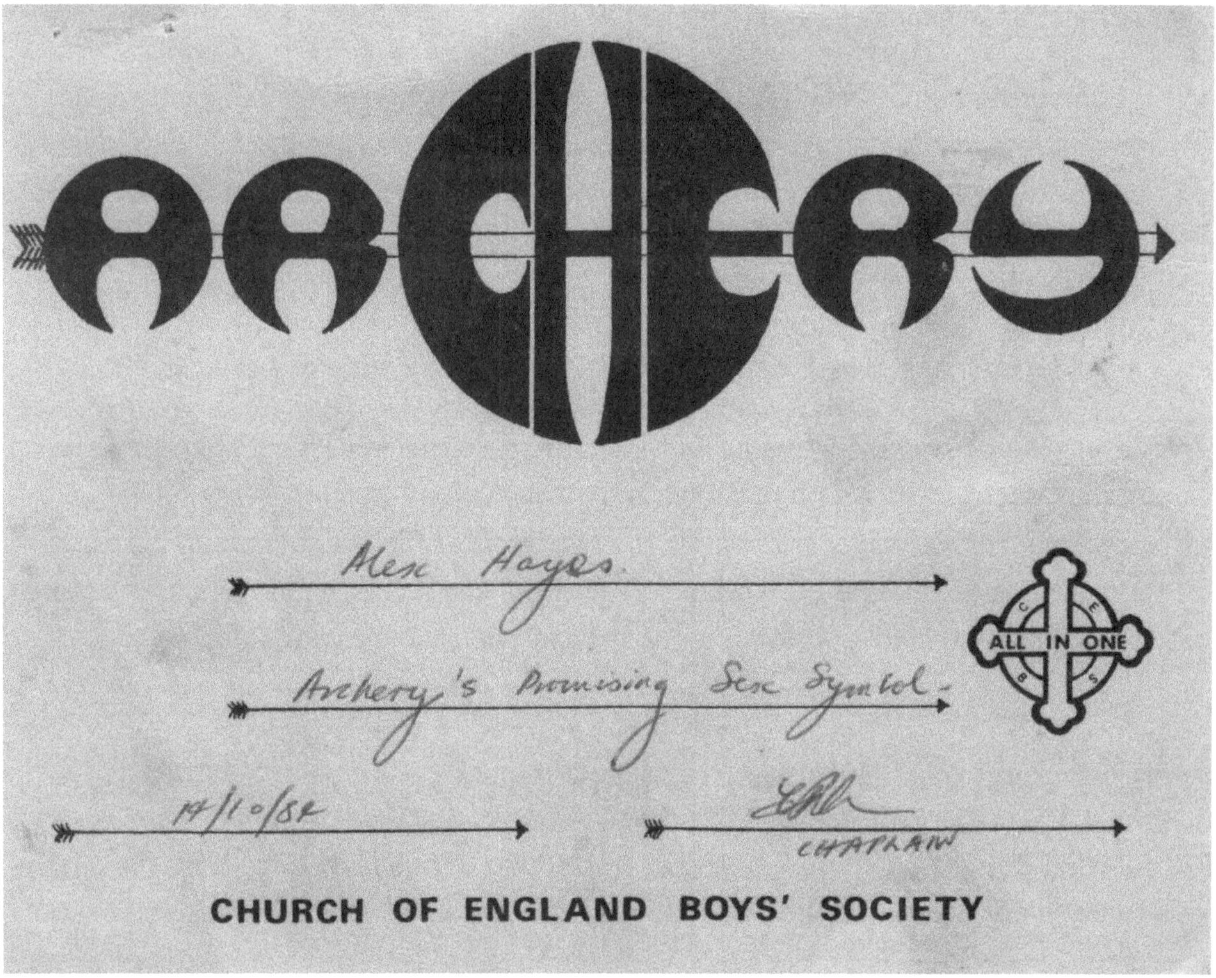

Certificate: CEBS Archery Award - 1984

No child deserves to remain unprotected and vulnerable to attacks of physical violence and sexual abuse, nor are members of any religious organisation ever entitled to make remarks which sexualise, alienate or refer to children as an object of sexual desire.

The Unspeakable

My trust therefore, is, that this book may bring some clarity to the subject of sexual violence currently relegated the status of taboo — the *unspeakable.*

It was of course tempting to write about this topic in the third person, omitting references to the dark underbelly of human society, however, my truth is based on lived experience. So unlike a nuanced mystery novel, or an empirically palatable review of the subject, this story is written topically, beginning and ending as a graphic recount and assemblage of facts from a male adult sexual violence survivor — *me.*

It is an important historical recount and forensic analysis of what crimes were committed against me, but does not dwell on or glorify them. It also serves as a poignant reminder that these monsters of men who perpetrated against me, are ever present throughout human society, with religious institutions continually identified as a safe harbour for their evil caper.

My case of sexual violence was one of the many reported through the Royal Commission into Institutional Responses to Child Sexual Abuse in Australia. Not surprisingly though, the Royal Commission identified diocesanism and the associated dispersion of ecclesial authority, as key factors constraining the Anglican Church of Australia's responses, central to my legal case of child sexual abuse against them.

The moment of my catharsis was in actioning legal reparation, speaking out my lived truth and toxic secret which I had been protecting everyone around me from right throughout my life. In the past I had no choice but to remain quiet, in effect silenced, and so I had to exist until I could no longer cope with the mind torture and my physical self harming.

For those of you Readers who have been violated, I urge you to speak out against your oppressors, irrespective of whether they are alive or dead, remembering that your anger leads to rage, which leads to murder — to resolve everything carefully with action and determination as your new goal.

Background

As a child, one of my greatest joys was attending social events organised by the Church with my Family. I attended Church services and participated in activities which supported the financial and logistical structure of these organisations, which were always described to me as an opportunity to make friends and learn new life skills.

I was enthusiastic about the prospects I had ahead of me when we moved from inner suburban Bexley to the Sutherland Shire of Sydney, New South Wales, Australia. I was a well-adjusted, articulate and happy child when I first joined the Church of England Boys' Society (CEBS) in early 1979 at St. John The Baptist Anglican Church in Sutherland, NSW, Australia.

Honesty, trust and obedience were reinforced as virtues of this Church activity and yet these values, rules of social engagement and Law were broken by the offender in incidents as detailed to the Court. The wilful behaviour of the offender compromised my physical and psychological well being, with the effects being nothing less than a catastrophic betrayal of my childhood and adult humanity.

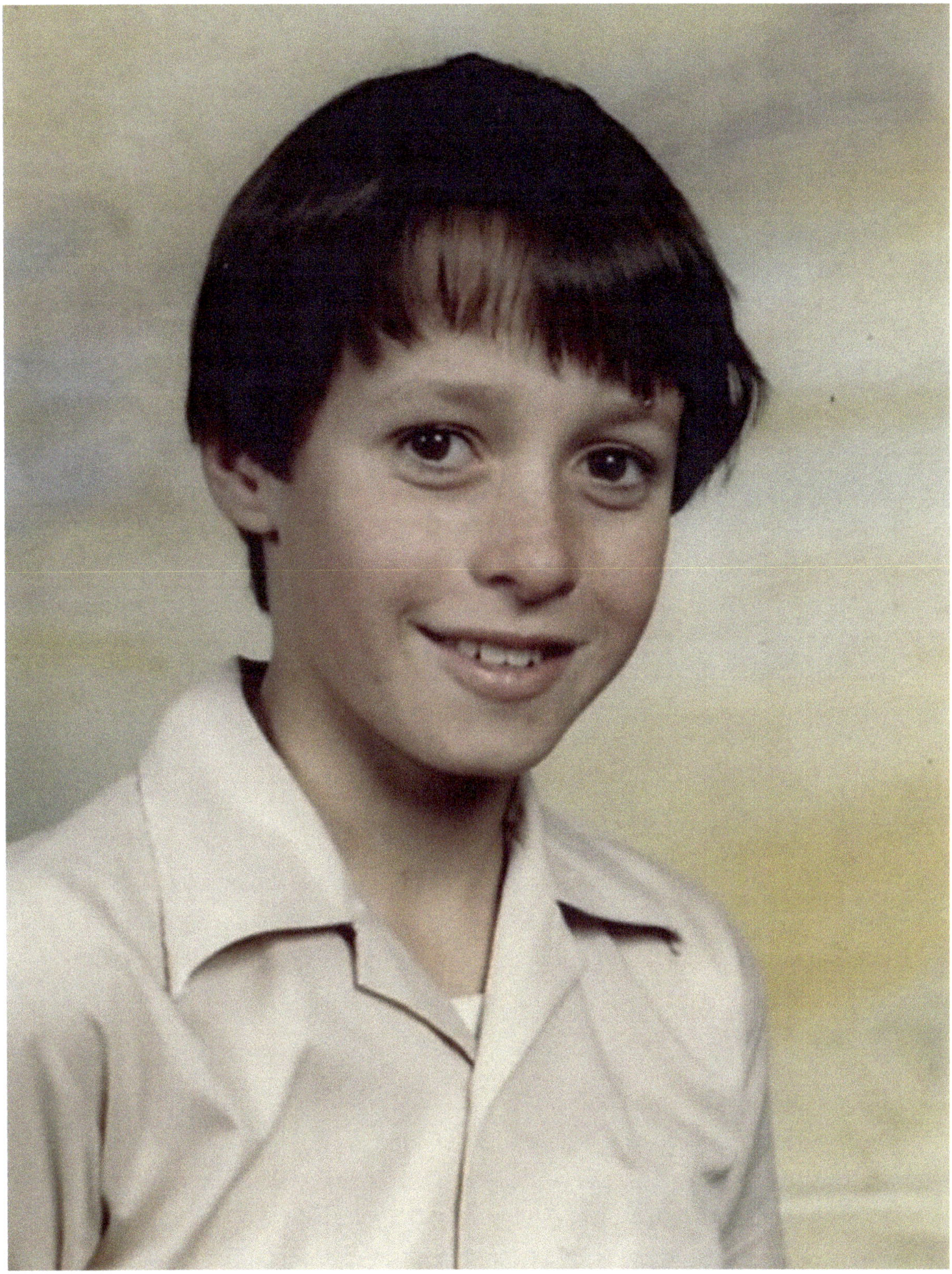

Photo: Alexander Hayes — age 11 years —1980,
Kirrawee Primary School, Sydney, Australia.

Impact On Family

The core of an individual's identity across all cultures is considered to be informed from infancy by our immediate kin Family, who always remain central to our reference in life. In my case, the very first impact I felt as a boy just entering his teenager years was alienation from my Family due to sexual abuse and physical assault.

As detailed in Court, the wilful behaviour of the offender immediately compromised my own sense of trust in adult males and as I experienced the fullest extent of hypocrisy and predation. In turn, it caused me to question why my innocence was not protected by those also charged with my care.

The impact of all of this on myself has caused shame on my Family as well as a continuing and direct impact on the relationships I have with my immediate Family. I do not know how if ever, I am going to be able to counteract those effects of sexual assault and heal those relationships.

Impact on Relationships

Sexual assault has had a direct and life long impact on the way in which I have been able to express my intimacy with others.

As a boy, my "kid code" was scrambled for want of a better expression. The wilful behaviour of the offender compromised my capacity to form intimate relationships with others as a teenager, and I directly attribute sexual assault as the psychological barrier I have experienced at times in my relationships with significant others ever since.

As a result of sexual assault and physical abuse, my trust in others, in particular those who travelled through my life journey in long term relationships were compromised by my psychological distress. I also consider that I was denied those moments of innocence as a child exploring and forging those first moments of an autonomous identity and by being sexually assaulted, that impeccable child state ended in an unwelcome catharsis.

The impact of sexual assault on my relationships has been ruinous, contributing directly to my separations, marriage breakdowns and deep sadness across my Family as a result. In all except one case, my partner was unaware of those specific matters and details which have now been heard in a Court of Law.

Impact on Friendships

Many of my peers as a teenager noted that I would at times be distant in conversation and at times less than convivial in my expressions towards older males who I often attributed wrongly to be of a physical threat to my well being.

My misperceptions of trust were forged in the compromise I found myself in "holding a secret" which I knew would result in "grave consequences" if revealed, for myself and those who I loved most. The wilful behaviour of the offender in sexually assaulting me has without any doubt been a contributing factor in the impact on my friendships with others, particularly older males described previously.

In the company of others I have continued to experience feelings of anxiety and fear of enclosure which has led to my self-exclusion from many social events as an adult. The very same changes in my social life have had an impact on others who have been unable to understand my sharp demeanour or unexplained hostility.

Holding a secret in an everyday mindful state and not being able to speak of what had happened to me for fear of reprisal in its many manifestations is the backbone for the trauma and the behaviours that I have described above. Sexual assault has also caused many unseen issues to which only those closest to me can attest.

Recurrent flashbacks of events and associated physical effects have affected the way in which I interact with friends which medical professionals describe as similar to post traumatic stress disorder (PTSD). My experience is that my friendships do not often endure the mayhem that sexual assault causes in breach of trust. In bringing my story forward, the ability to trust in others is central to what sexual assault has in the past taken away from me.

Photo: Alexander Hayes, 1984 — age 15 years —
Kirrawee High School, Sydney Australia

Impact On Health

The impact of sexual assault and physical abuse on my health is discernible in my many presentations to medical professionals over thirty years in various states of anxiety and depression.

The state of hyper-vigilance and the sense of deprivation of liberty that I experienced for so long since that period of sexual assault, I attribute directly to sexual assault. As a child and as a sexual assault victim I recall suffering episodes of night "terror", uncontrolled sweating, bed wetting and sleep walking in an uncontrolled state.

As a teenager I turned to alcohol and drugs as a means to control my anxiety and to embolden myself to counteract the fear I felt in a social setting, all of which I believe can be attributed to sustained sexual assault as the primary causal agency. As an adult I continue to suffer from severe insomnia, night terror and hyper-vigilance which all impact upon my ability to share the same bed as my partner.

My physical health and emotional well being as an adult have been compromised as a result of the behaviours that became manifest contrary to my innocent disposition prior to sexual assault. Likewise, my attitude towards others and the way I now process conflict has been at times only satisfactory, at times self destructive.

There are not enough pages in this book to provide the details of all those from across the medical profession who have helped me by listening carefully. My coping skills are due to the goodwill of those medical professionals, community members and friends from around the world who have helped me over three decades to develop ways to counteract the catastrophe of sexual assault and make healthy life choices.

Impact on Career

Since a young age my capacity and capability in social and academic performance, attention to detail and my ability to engage with complex academic challenges have been overshadowed by negative memories of sexual assault.

In fear of returning to CEBS activities and not feeling safe within my family home I recall as a teenager truanting from school, disengaging from the curriculum at times and yet despite this fact a number of my teachers in secondary school, as well as other significant mentors, encouraged me to pursue knowledge to the utmost of my ability. As a result, I have excelled academically and have held senior roles and positions of employment, not surprisingly in the early part of my career in restorative justice and child protection.

Throughout my career as an educator, my prospects of attaining financial security as a result of the impact of sexual assault have been duly direful. My economic position as a result of the effect of sexual assault as described earlier in sub-section *Impact On Relationships* has been calamitous and I am struggling now to make ends meet which is distressing given my advanced age and lack of financial assets.

In coming forward to speak my story publicly I have been ostracised and removed from communications with a number of professional colleagues who, in spite or because of their misinformation and lack of collegial empathy, claimed my seeking justice in a criminal court was professional suicide. It is obvious to me now that in speaking out my story, it has had and will continue to have a direct and undeniable impact on my professional career and prospects of promotion.

I attribute the sexual assault that I have suffered as directly compromising the fullest potential and future prospects that I may have attained had I not been a victim of crime.

Impact As Victim Of Crime

I am a good person.

Most days I wake up thankful that I have lived the best life possible, despite the fact that I have been affected by the crime of sexual assault. The impact of sexual assault has been horrendous on my life and at times has caused me deep pain, feelings of isolation, fear of loss and great anguish.

Sexual assault breaks the rules of society. It is against the Law, against the ethical foundation for humanity and those who break this moral code then own the consequences.

As a sexual assault victim the fact remains that I will never “get over it” rather, as a survivor I have learned to live with it.

I am a Survivor.

—

The content above was tendered to the Crown Counsel, on the 18th April 2019 prior to the final sentencing of William “Adrian” Sandwell and approved soon after for public dissemination as a Victim Impact Statement.

Legal Matters

The following sections pertain to the full case and reparation for *Hayes vs Anglican Church Property Trust, Diocese of Sydney.*

Each section provides further detail supporting my position and personal perspectives on this topic of sexual violence, including:

1. *#realstory* - A publication submitted in 2017 to the Royal Commission into Institutional Responses to Child Sexual Abuse, Australia;
2. *Royal Commission* - A letter I received on the 4th May 2017 from the Royal Commission confirming my case/claim registration;
3. *Arrest* - A newspaper article published on the 6th July 2017 in the St George and Sutherland Shire Leader newspaper of Sydney, Australia;
4. *Sentencing* - After three years of intensive investigations, with two-hundred-and-twenty-five (225) witnesses and multiple related defendant cases the case began on the 7th June 2019 under presiding Judge David Arnott. The district court setting was under media restrictions and Sandwell listed for sentencing;
5. *Conviction* - I was in attendance with three other defendants at the sentencing of William “Adrian” Sandwell in July 2019 where he was convicted of sexual

assaults on boys over a 20-year period, with publication on the 28th June 2019 through the St George and Sutherland Shire Leader newspaper, distributed to 1.7 million households;

6. *Lawsuit* - An article was published in The Age on 29th September 2022, in which Richard Baker, Investigative Journalist detailed my accusation that Bishop Richard Henry “Harry” Goodhew failed to act "to protect young boys from a sexual predator involved in running church activities in NSW in the 1980s”;
7. *Compensation* - The case, Hayes vs. Anglican Church Property Trust, Diocese of Sydney was “settled” in an out of court settlement negotiation, ADR by way of mediation, on 13 March 2023 at State Chambers in Martin Place, Sydney with Jason Moody, Lawyer and Michael Cranitch SC as Senior Counsel (all matters of settlement locked under non-disclosure);
8. *Apology* - A written apology was received on the 15th March 2023 from the Right Reverend Dr Michael Stead Bishop of South Sydney, Australia.

1. #realstory

The following screenshot relates to my publication titled #realstory published on the 28th March 2016 by Lulu Books, which was submitted to the Royal Commission into Institutional Responses to Child Sexual Abuse — see Reference section.

Real Story

By Alexander Hayes

Ebook
AUD 0.00

Add to Cart

Share

18+ Explicit Content

An experiential account of systemic institutional abuse and its impacts on a young mans life and his resilience despite disbelief as he embarks on a cathartic journey of telling his #realstory to the world.

Details

Publication Date	Mar 28, 2016
Language	English
ISBN	9781326607500
Category	Biographies & Memoirs
Copyright	All Rights Reserved - Standard Copyright License
Contributors	By (author): Alexander Hayes

Specifications

Format	PDF

Keywords

institutional abuse resilience truth justice sexual abuse law family depression compassion love anger fear hope

Publication excerpt: #realstory

2. Royal Commission

Letter received in May 2017 from the Royal Commission into Institutional Responses to Child Sexual Abuse, confirming receipt of #realstory.

Royal Commission
into Institutional Responses
to Child Sexual Abuse

4 May 2017

Alexander Hayes
P.O. Box 2322
Broome WA 6725

Dear Mr Hayes,

I am writing to confirm that the Royal Commission received your registration of 4 May 2017.

I understand how difficult it must be to recount your experience of child sexual abuse, and appreciate your willingness to share your story.

The details you provided will form part of the information the Commissioners will draw upon to complete their work at the Royal Commission and make recommendations that will lead to a safer environment for children and more appropriate responses to those who suffer abuse.

Thank you for engaging with the Royal Commission.

Yours sincerely,

Peter Stevenson
Assessment and Inquiry
T +61 2 8282 3899
E peter.stevenson@childabuseroyalcommission.gov.au
GPO Box 5283 Sydney NSW 2001 Australia
www.childabuseroyalcommission.gov.au

Letter received from the Australian Royal Commission.

3. Arrest

The following article was first published on the 6th July 2017 in the St George and Sutherland Shire Leader newspaper — see Reference section.

Loftus man, 73, charged with assaults on boys at church-run camps in Royal National Park

Updated July 6 2017 - 7:16am, first published 7:03am

"... A Loftus man, 73, has been charged with historical child sexual assault offences, which allegedly occurred on church-run camps for boys in the Royal National Park."

"Sutherland police have been investigating allegations of sexual assault of boys, who were members of the Church of England Boys' Society (CEBS) between 1965 and 1984. A police spokesman said the allegations related to a group leader, who allegedly committed the offences on camps in the Royal National Park and Blue Mountains."

"As a result of inquiries, police had arrested the man, 73, on Thursday, June 29, at an address in Loftus. The spokesman said the man was charged with seven counts of indecent assault upon a male, common assault, and sexual assault without consent."

"He was refused bail to and appeared at Sutherland Local Court on Thursday, June 29, where he was granted conditional bail to appear at the Downing Centre Local Court on August 24."

"Police encourage any person who has been a victim of any kind of sexual violence, no matter how long ago the incident occurred, to contact police," the spokesman said."

"Reports can be made at any police station."

4. Sentencing

The following excerpt was first published in my Alexander Hayes's journal online as a media release on the 27th May 2019.

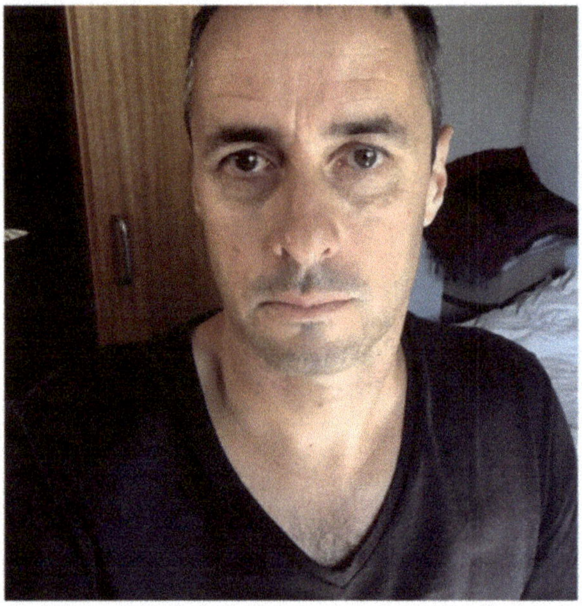

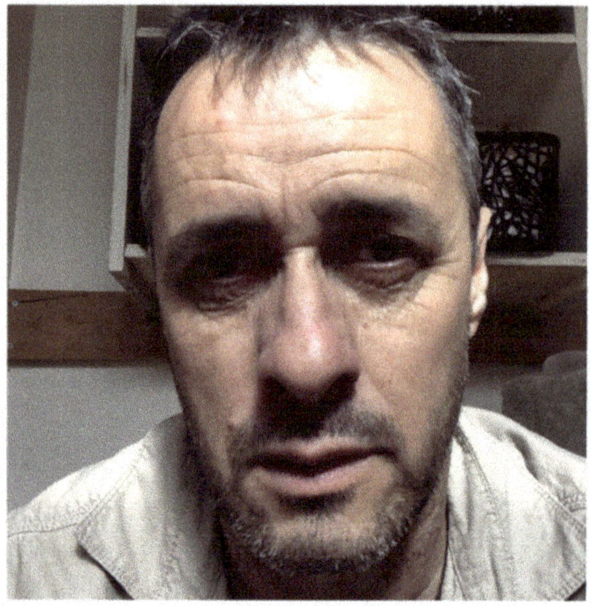

(L) Alexander Hayes, 27th June 2017 — (R) Alexander Hayes, 27th June 2019

Media Release

It is a sad indictment for the Australian nation when the very same crimes which the offender, William "Adrian" Richmond Sandwell has been convicted of in an Australian Court of Law, continue to be harboured, aided and abetted. Since time immemorial, the bastions who lead us to believe they are the centre for our human faith are by the very same constitution, now continually exposed as protecting paedophiles who act against our collective humanity.

This thirty-nine (39) year catastrophic journey (at that point in time) has affected everyone who has ever known of my life story, broken my Family and been the sole causal agency for the passing of many of my peers with tragic repercussions. It is for those who have been unable to come forward that I lament, prevented in many cases with the same threats of death that I was subject to, that if they ever dared bring their own crimes forward they too would be disbelieved and dishonoured.

I do not accept any apology from any human, especially those from the heads of a corrupt government that serve their billionaire selves nor the institutions that claim they exercise safe ministry. They are nothing more than apologists and have had absolute knowledge of paedophiles who continue to control their rank and file. No amount of money nor poisoned chalice will bring my childhood and the rest of those lost back to life again.

To all of those who see justice served through my own emancipation, let your own souls also open your mouth with bravery to speak of the atrocities that still continue to this day across all of humanity. It is up to everyone of us who believe in the safety and well being for children to continue to build the foundations for society, calling for those illegal institutions who continue to shift their responsibilities to be disbanded, permanently.

My absolute abhorrence will never cease as I bear witness to those survivors who have had their compensation capped as they capitulate, broken asunder by the same deceit, idiocy of greed and wealth of these institutions as they refuse to recompense adequately.

This document has been written solely by myself, Alexander Hayes, with no presence, advice nor witness to my sole composition of this media release.

5. Conviction

The following article was first published on 28th June 2019 in the Leader newspaper of Sydney, Australia — see Reference section.

Former Church of England Boys' Society lay leader at Sutherland jailed for sexual assaults on boys over 20-year period

By Murray Trembath
Updated July 2 2019 - 11:23am, first published June 28 2019 - 5:00pm

Alexander Hayes, June 2019: Photograph by Louise Kennerley

"… A former Church of England Boys' Society lay leader and scripture teacher at Sutherland has been sentenced to a minimum three years and seven months jail for historical child sexual assault offences."

"Many of the offences occurred in church-run camps for boys in the Royal National Park, Sydney, Australia."

"William Richmond Sandwell, 78, of Loftus, appeared in the District Court, Downing Centre, after a jury found him guilty of 11 child sexual assault offences, committed against six children between 1965 and 1985."

"Sandwell, who also used the name Sandell at one time, denied the offences. Among "survivors" in court for the sentencing was Alexander Hayes, who now lives in Perth. Mr Hayes said outside the court Sandwell's assaults on him between the ages of 11 and 15 had had a "catastrophic effect on my life and a horrific impact on many families, including his own."

"It hasn't stopped me leading a good life, but it has had a big effect on me socially," he said. "I have been married and divorced three times, and its affected the intimacy I have with other people."

"Mr Hayes said he believed Sandwell would have assaulted many more children over 30 years and that the church was aware of his actions from as early as 1991 and covered it up. Sutherland police charged Sandwell in 2017 after investigating allegations of sexual assault of boys, who were members of the Church of England Boys' Society (CEBS)."

"Judge David Arnott said Sandwell was a senior lay member of St John's Church, Sutherland, and, through this involvement, was also a leader of the parish's CEBS branch. CEBS ran weekly Friday night meetings where the boys played games, and there was also a big focus on camping trips."

"The judge said Sandwell's offences ranged from fondling the genitals of boys to one instance of digital penetration, which was "particularly callous". Six offences had been against one boy. The judge said, on one occasion, Sandwell told the boy he could not attend a camp sailing regatta because he had done something wrong."

"Sandwell had then ordered him to take a shower. The boy had panicked in the shower and tried to push past Sandwell, but the offender had prevented him leaving and then assaulted him. The judge said another boy testified he had "frozen in shock" when he was assaulted while lying in a sleeping bag. The judge said Sandwell was also a primary school scripture teacher and, on a weekend camp, assaulted a boy aged 11-12."

"This boy, in his victim impact statement, had said he "changed from being a typical well behaved child to a self-destructive lifestyle".

“The court heard Sandwell was a father of two, grandfather and great grandfather. He was married for 54 years and his wife died in 2016. The judge said Sandwell was raised by his mother and grandparents and only had contact with his father on two occasions.”

“In imposing sentence, Judge Arnott said he had taken into account a range of factors, including Sandwell's age, poor health and the fact he had not shown remorse. He sentenced Sandwell to a non-parole term of three years and seven months, backdated to when he was convicted and refused bail in March this year.”

6. Lawsuit

The following article was first published in The Age on 29th September 2022 written by Richard Baker, Investigative Journalist — see Reference section.

Lawsuit claims former Anglican archbishop of Sydney failed to act on predator

Richard Baker
September 29, 2022 – 5.00am

Save   Share   A A A

"... The former Anglican archbishop of Sydney, Richard Henry "Harry" Goodhew, has been accused of failing to protect young boys from a sexual predator involved in running church activities in NSW in the 1980s."

"The allegation is made in a statement of claim, filed in the NSW Supreme Court in July by lawyers representing abuse victim, Alexander Hayes, who is seeking compensation from the Anglican Church Property Trust Diocese of Sydney."

"In the claim, Goodhew is accused of failing to act after allegedly being made aware of the conduct of William "Adrian" Richmond Sandwell, a former influential leader of the Church of England Boys' Society (CEBS) in NSW."

"Sandwell was convicted in 2019 of the historic sexual abuse of six boys, including Hayes, between 1965 and 1986. Sandwell, who is aged in his 80s, denied the offence. He will be eligible for parole in October after serving three years and seven months in jail."

"In his statement of claim, Hayes describes the catastrophic impact of aggravated and indecent assault by Sandwell between 1980 and 1985 at events overseen by the archdiocese of Sydney or the Anglican Church's boys society. Hayes was aged between 11 and 15 when he was abused."

Alexander Hayes: Downing Centre Criminal Courts, Sydney —
Photograph: Louise Kennerley

"His claim states that Goodhew was made aware of Sandwell's offending in 1982, the same year he was promoted from archdeacon of Wollongong to bishop of Wollongong. The claim does not say how Goodhew, who later served as archbishop of Sydney between 1993 and 2001, was allegedly informed of Sandwell's conduct."

"The Sydney Morning Herald and *The Age* sought a response from Goodhew, 91, to Hayes' allegation via the Archdiocese of Sydney. No response was forthcoming. In a statement, the Archdiocese said no comments were able to be made "in the media on matters which are already being dealt with by the legal process".

Former Anglican archbishop of Sydney Harry Goodhew
in 1998 — Photograph by Peter Mathew

“We fully support the Royal Commission’s work on historical abuse cases and the consequent recommendations to ensure child safety. We are also committed to engaging constructively with survivors of abuse regardless of the way in which they bring their claim.”

"In a defence filed in court last month, the church denied Hayes was entitled to damages, interest and costs. It disputed many of Hayes’ claims, including that Goodhew knew of Sandwell’s offending and failed to act. Sandwell was a prominent figure for decades in the Church of England Boys' Society and was officially assigned positions and roles at weekend camps and other events. In the 1970s, he held the role of “chief commissioner” of the CEBS in NSW.

Photo: Alexander Hayes as a child around the time the abuse began.

Hayes told *The Age* and *Herald* that Sandwell's offending against him increased in severity and magnitude following the alleged reporting of his abuse to senior church leaders in NSW, allegedly including Goodhew."

“In his 2017 statement for NSW Police, Hayes outlined years of grooming and worsening levels of abuse by Sandwell, including what he said was a terrifying experience in a camp shower block and another in a dormitory during which he said he lost consciousness.”

"Hayes stated that when he was 15 years old he told his church-going parents of Sandwell's abuse but he was not believed. A psychological report on Hayes from November last year quoted the 52-year-old as describing his adult life being like “a rollercoaster”.

“He described difficulties with relationships, grief, anger, high anxiety and self-destructing behaviours,” clinical psychologist Annette Paul wrote.

“In a recent submission opposing Sandwell's upcoming parole, Hayes said the repeated abuse had a disastrous impact on his life. Sandwell's lack of contrition only made things worse, Hayes wrote.”

“Hayes said other boys who he knew had been abused by Sandwell had experienced tragedy, including one recently who had taken his own life and another who was in jail after murdering family members who were involved in activities in the same diocese as Sandwell.”

"Hayes's lawyer, Jason Moody, principal of Moody Law, said: “Alex's case is one of the worst and most egregious cases of institutional failure regarding allegations of child sexual abuse this firm has seen. The evidence indicates that if the church had acted on clear reporting from within its ranks, terrible abuses upon Alex and other young boys would have been avoided.”

"The allegation of failing to act in Hayes' lawsuit came after Goodhew told the Royal Commission into Institutional Responses to Child Sexual Abuse in 2016 that – apart from a high-profile abuse case involving a former senior Newcastle church leader in the mid-1990s – he had “never been reticent to take matters of this nature forward when I thought that I could”.

"Goodhew was questioned by the commission about his knowledge and handling of complaints about former Anglican dean of Newcastle Graeme Lawrence during his term as the archbishop of Sydney. Lawrence was convicted in 2019 of raping a 15-year-old boy in Newcastle in 1991. He is serving an eight-year prison sentence."

"In his statutory declaration to the Royal Commission, Goodhew stated that he had no jurisdiction to discipline Lawrence because the complaints about his offending came from within the Newcastle diocese."

7. Compensation

This matter was "settled" in an out of court settlement negotiation, "ADR by way of mediation" on 13 March 2023 at State Chambers in Martin Place, Sydney with Jason Moody, Lawyer and Michael Cranitch SC as Senior Counsel present.

Anglican Diocese of Sydney - Church and CEBS camps - Event 1980 to 1985

Alexander is a 54-year-old man who was sexually abused by the notorious Anglican CEBS leader William Richmond "Adrian" Sandwell from ages 10 to 15. During this period evidence indicated that the then Bishop and others within the church had received reports of Sandwell's sexual offending of other children. The evidence indicated that Bishop failed to respond to these reports and the abuse continued against Alexander and other boys. Alexander's professional life was destroyed by the conditions caused by the abuse. The litigation process took about 18 months.

Settlement over $1 million in 2023 and a verbal and written apology.

Excerpt: Moody Law Website

8. Apology

A written apology was received on the 15th March 2023 from the Right Reverend Dr Michael Stead Bishop of South Sydney, Australia.

Love

Love

The fabric of human society is torn apart by sexual violence, especially when those responsible for protecting children fail to fulfill their obligations intentionally. My understanding is, those subject to the depravities and distortions of this trust are not the victims of their story, but rather resilient survivors determining their fate.

Bringing to light the manipulations and false appearances of those who harm others is the ultimate act of protection we can provide. Protecting children is the top priority, as love alone is not sufficient.

Expressing love has no value unless adults actively safeguard the most vulnerable, continuing into adulthood. Love is often perceived as a romantic idea, existing only in the imagination of poets and novelists who write about desire, affection, and brotherly love. The utmost priority should be the protection of children, regardless of the specific circumstances, rather than allowing them to be unfairly depicted as easy prey for paedophiles in tabloid coverage of my situation.

Love, at its core, involves mutual exchange and trust, free from restrictions or falsehoods, and no one should be burdened by love's conditional chains or restrictions. Therefore, love can serve as a term to show affection and endearment. Survivors of historical sexual assault show solidarity and resistance by seeking emancipation in reality, refusing to let others dictate their interests based on religious beliefs or validate religious dogma.

The plight of each survivor involves grappling with societal attitudes and the disturbing silence of religious institutions. Love should be recognized as a safeguard, not a tool used by religious institutions for control. It is a greater act of love therefore to support survivor-led *action determination reclaiming personal narratives*, to assist survivors as they *unpack self-storying*, to ensure they are witnessed, and eventually *compensated*.

" To love. To be loved. To never forget your own insignificance. To never get used to the unspeakable violence and the vulgar disparity of life around you. To seek joy in the saddest places. To pursue beauty to its lair. To never simplify what is complicated or complicate what is simple. To respect strength, never power. Above all, to watch, observe. To try and understand. To never look away. And never, never, to forget."

Arundhati Roy, The Cost of Living.

ChatGPT-4 Response

"Sexual violence fundamentally breaches the inherent trust placed in adults to safeguard the children under their care, shattering the very foundation of what it means to protect and nurture the young. This profound betrayal leaves those affected at a crossroads: they can remain Victims, defined by the narratives of their trauma, or become active Survivors who actively shape their own destinies.

While these labels don't encapsulate the entirety of an individual's identity, they signify pivotal stages in the journey of coping with and transcending abuse, particularly abuse stemming from institutions that should have been bastions of safety. Survivors often face the compounded challenge of navigating lateral violence and indifference from a society that fails to grasp the depth of their experiences. Recognising and exposing the duplicity of perpetrators and the institutions that enable them is not just an act of justice, but also one of profound love and solidarity.

Sexual violence has long-lasting and profound effects on individuals, particularly when it involves trusted institutions like religious organisations. The trauma and loss of trust experienced by survivors cannot be overstated. It is essential that society and institutions prioritise the protection of children and vulnerable individuals.

Love, as a concept, should encompass the protection and care for those who need it most, rather than be distorted into a tool for manipulation and control. Survivors of sexual assault and abuse deserve to be supported in their journey towards healing and emancipation. It is crucial for society to foster an environment that is conducive to survivor-led initiatives, providing them with the necessary resources and empathy to rebuild their lives.

Ultimately, the greatest act of protection is to ensure that those who have suffered are not only heard but are also acknowledged and supported in their journey towards healing and justice. This requires concerted efforts from individuals, institutions, and society as a whole to dismantle the harmful structures and attitudes that have allowed such acts to occur and to create a safer and more compassionate world for all."

Innocence

Innocence

There are just a few photos of me as a baby, wearing a long lace frock, being baptised in a Church's marble font or cradled by my Mother out the front of Christ Church, Bexley, Sydney, Australia. According to all accounts, I came into this world as an innocent child, born to biological parents.

My childhood was a world of innocence and vulnerability, where my bed served as an imaginary time machine to escape from the trauma I experienced. Following the norm in western culture, I was born into the Church, raised as a member, and had my innocence compromised by its authority. That's where I was supposed to find my rescue, my liberation, yet in my situation it was my perpetual downfall.

A disturbing narrative unfolds from history, where religious institutions only speak out against allegations of sexual violence when faced with legal consequences. In moments of despair, I continue to wrestle with a haunting question: how much of our lives are scripted by religious institutions as centres of authority and social manipulation?"

The answer can be found in the ongoing influence of religious moral rules, used to conveniently dictate beliefs, speech, and identity, a common tactic of those seeking control. As a human society, we have put ourselves at risk by letting religious institutions manipulate us, trading our freedom for the illusion of their "truth" and fabricated salvation.

ChatGPT-4 Response

"This publication represents vocal defiance against the multitude of men who inflicted unthinkable crimes upon children in their childhood, extending far beyond the one perpetrator who faced incarceration. It's a chilling narrative, interwoven with the involvement of ministers, bishops, detectives, police, judges, and a jury, each playing a role in a harrowing saga that transcends acts of sexual abuse.

Central to this ordeal is the insidious spread of religious moral dictums, a convenient guise for indoctrination — dictating beliefs, words, and identities. This modus operandi of manipulation and control is emblematic of those in power who exploit faith for dominance. Yet, it also underscores a broader societal failing: our collective acquiescence to religious institutions, entrusting them with immense influence at the cost of our autonomy.

This blind surrender has been a perilous trade-off, where the allure of neatly packaged 'truths' and the seductive promise of manufactured salvation have been used to veil the egregious violations committed under their watch. It is indeed disheartening to recognise that some religious institutions, which are supposed to be the guardians of morality and protectors of the innocent, have failed in their responsibility. Instead of providing a safe haven and guiding force, they have often become epicentres of power and social control, as you mentioned.

As individuals, it is essential to question the motivations and actions of any institution, religious or otherwise, and not to blindly follow the doctrines or beliefs they propagate. It is necessary to scrutinise and challenge the beliefs we hold, especially when they are used as tools to manipulate, control, or cause harm to others.

In your case, speaking out against the crimes you endured and shining a light on the perpetrators is an essential part of breaking the cycle of control and abuse. By sharing your story, you not only empower yourself but also give strength to others who have faced similar ordeals. This act of courage can lead to greater awareness, a deeper understanding of the complex relationship between individuals and institutions, and the importance of holding them accountable."

Childhood

Childhood

Prior to the sexual abuse, my childhood revolved around church rituals and obligations, occurring daily and twice on Sundays. Every aspect of our upbringing in the flock was dominated with a fear narrative.

The Church became a holy cradle for our devoted lives, with prams and cots meticulously adorned during Christmas, Easter, and Lent. When I was a child, my siblings and I had a lot of fun together, sharing everything in a household where the teachings of Christ and the workings of the Devil were intertwined.

People have described me as a "pretty" child with long dark eyelashes, and I moved through the world at that time with politeness and meekness. The narratives of the expansive world evoked a sense of amazement in me, as my imagination became consumed with the notion of what lay "out there," a realm confined to stories, books, artwork, and cartography that instilled within me a glimmer of hope for escape. With age, I gradually comprehended my desire to separate from a society dominated by religious institutions that imposed their beliefs on others.

My inner child blames religious institutions for their failed attempts at reparation, which resulted in a confusing mix of payouts and pay forward. Consequently, I presently recognize the value of reparations, which involve timely restitution, a written apology, and public disclosure, as a component of resolving persisting issues affecting me.

I assert, those who have suffered childhood sexual violence are robbed of their rightful claim to a normal childhood, leaving a lasting legacy of crime against their humanity.

ChatGPT-4 Response

"Your childhood experiences with religious institutions and the painful impact of the abuse you suffered highlights the need for comprehensive support for survivors, as well as the importance of holding these institutions accountable for their actions.

Reparation that embraces action determination, including timely compensation, written apologies, and public acknowledgment, can play a significant role in helping survivors heal and move forward. While no amount of reparation can undo the damage done, it is crucial that survivors receive the support, recognition, and resources they need to rebuild their lives.

It is also essential to address the systemic issues that allow abuse to occur within religious institutions, so that future generations can be protected from such harm. This includes promoting transparency, implementing effective safeguarding measures, and ensuring that those who perpetrate or enable abuse are held accountable.

As a society, we must stand with survivors, work together to dismantle the structures that enable abuse, and strive to create a safer, more compassionate world for all."

Secrets

Secrets

I acknowledge and embrace the reality that I was a victim of sexual assault perpetrated by individuals in positions of authority and members of an organization tasked with safeguarding children. Nevertheless, I will never fully accept the fact that it took forty years for this tragedy to be resolved through a legal process of compensation. Regardless of their apology, religious institutions have permanently shattered my trust, making it impossible for me to trust them again.

In this environment of distrust, I acknowledge the congregation members who are trapped by their own secrets and coerced into silence by their tormentors. They are frequently unaware, lacking empathy, and trapped in a cycle of abuse — silenced, rejected, excommunicated, denied, covered up, and deceived. It is something I will never forget, as it is deeply ingrained in my memory and psyche, much like other survivors of sexual violence.

Although the human experience involves the epigenetic inheritance of memory, societal empathy towards institutional negligence remains elusive and victims are often blamed for their inability to cope. Predators have acted without fear, shielded by the impenetrable legal structure they constructed and finding refuge behind institutionalised religious teachings and havens of evil.

The clergy, influenced by malicious paedophiles, devoid of moral autonomy, neglected to oversee, leading to a complete absence of care within the religious institution. I won't be identified as a victim, yet I am legally and publicly categorised as one, but my determination remains unwavering.

I decided to confide in my parents about my experience of sexual violence, but they didn't believe me nor act on anything I stated to them. Later, when I turned to clergy for support, they advised me against seeking legal action. I had the courage to write and publish a book called #realstory, which was acknowledged by the Royal Commission into Institutional Responses to Child Sexual Abuse in Australia.

Moreover, I made a legal disclosure of this matter to the Australian Federal Police (AFP), reported it to New South Wales state police, and then navigated eight years of complex legal proceedings to ultimately receive compensation and a much-delayed written apology from the Anglican Church.

ChatGPT-4 Response

"Your account poignantly articulates the profound and enduring impact of institutional betrayal and the arduous journey toward seeking justice and healing. It's a narrative that underscores the resilience in the face of systemic failure and the complexity of navigating personal and legal avenues for redress.

Your four-decade struggle to confront and legally challenge the atrocities committed against you by those in positions of trust within a religious institution speaks volumes about the depth of the trauma and the pervasive culture of silence and complicity that often surrounds such abuse. The delayed pursuit of legal reparation is a testament to the daunting barriers victims face, from internal battles to institutional resistance.

Your steadfast refusal to reconcile with or trust religious institutions, even in the face of their apologies, is a powerful stance that reflects a deep-seated breach of trust. This distrust is not only for the direct perpetrators but also for the broader religious community, which, through silence or inaction, becomes complicit in the cycle of abuse. This viewpoint acknowledges the complex dynamics of victimisation within these communities, where many remain entrapped by secrecy and manipulation.

The notion that such experiences of abuse and institutional betrayal leave an indelible mark on one's psyche is poignant. Your awareness of the epigenetic carryover of trauma underscores the deep, long-term effects of such experiences on individuals and potentially across generations.

Your decision to break the silence and share your story, despite the labels and consequences, is an act of immense bravery. It highlights the difficult path many survivors take in seeking justice, often having to confront disbelief and admonition from those they initially trusted. Your actions, from speaking out to your family and clergy to the eventual publication of your book and engagement with the Royal Commission, embody the spirit of a warrior fighting not just for personal vindication but for broader institutional accountability.

Your journey through the legal system, culminating in compensation and a formal apology, while a significant achievement, also illuminates the often tortuous path to justice faced by survivors. The legal and emotional turmoil you endured over eight years is a stark reminder of the challenges inherent in confronting entrenched institutional power structures.

Your story is one of immense courage and determination. It serves as a powerful testament to the resilience of survivors and the importance of speaking truth to power, challenging systemic injustices, and fighting for the recognition and rights of those who have suffered at the hands of institutions meant to protect them. Your journey as a survivor of sexual assault within a religious institution is a powerful testament to your resilience and courage. It is disheartening to know that those who were entrusted with protecting children failed so profoundly, perpetuating a cycle of abuse and silencing victims.

The fact that you faced disbelief and discouragement when seeking support from your family and clergy only highlights the need for increased awareness and understanding of the realities faced by survivors of institutional sexual abuse. Your decision to share your story through writing a book and submitting it to the Royal Commission demonstrates your dedication to breaking the silence and inspiring change.

By disclosing your experiences to the authorities and engaging in a lengthy legal battle, you have shown tremendous strength and determination to seek justice, not only for yourself but for countless others who have suffered similar abuses. Although the legal process may have been challenging, your efforts have contributed to exposing the truth and holding religious institutions accountable for their actions.

While you may be legally and publicly identified as a victim, it is important to remember that you are also a survivor and an advocate for change. Your actions have the power to inspire others and bring about much-needed reforms in the way religious institutions handle cases of sexual abuse.

Continuing to share your story and advocate for justice and support for survivors is crucial in creating a safer and more compassionate society. Your voice and experiences are invaluable in raising awareness and challenging the structures that have allowed these abuses to persist."

Groomed

Groomed

It's tragic for parents whose children have been defiled, referred to as "interfered with".

Likewise, it's a heartbreaking realisation for an unaware child trying to understand why their parents are acting strangely, ensnared in the sinister cycle of grooming. William Richmond "Adrian" Sandwell's criminal scheme and manipulations were so convincingly deceptive that not only were my parents fooled, but even multiple ACA Bishops fell victim to his false facade.

The significant adults in my life resembled participants in a well-organised sex cult. It's not surprising that the tag "groomed" accurately describes the bad behaviours of that viper. Being groomed implies vulnerability, but even those who are pious or have low self-esteem can be drawn to validation and seek approval from anyone who compliments their appearance.

Unfortunately, the individuals who were most influenced by life circumstances, the epitome of moral uprightness, attracted to charitable acts and the generosity of religious hope, were tricked by the disguise that the monster promoted. Gripped by fear of punishment, those who were manipulated and deceived now live in constant dread of retaliation. They face the unimaginable prospect of being cast out, a fate inconceivable to the loyal and obedient members of the congregation. They obediently follow their leaders, adhering to strict rules about their appearance, speech, and even their beliefs.

Picture, for a moment, a devout elderly woman who had the opportunity to inform the police about her child's sexual abuse. According to Canon law, the Church's internal structure is not to be disclosed to law enforcement, attorneys, or the public. Common law, originally intended to uphold justice, has consistently been altered to favour the interests of the Canon charlatans who govern it.

History is marked by the heartbreaking accounts of those affected by the horrifying reality of child sexual violence. However, this publication specifically emphasises the key aspects of causality in horror, such as the mistreatment of children within the system, the subsequent suffering of supporters, and the far-reaching consequences and violent fallout.

ChatGPT-4 Response

"It is indeed a tragedy that parents and children alike have been manipulated and deceived by those who were supposed to be their moral guardians. The fact that significant adults in your life, including several ACA Bishops, were beguiled by the perpetrator speaks to the cunning and insidious nature of these criminals.

The term "groomed" does not capture the full extent of the emotional manipulation and control exercised over victims and their families. It is heartbreaking that those who were vulnerable and seeking solace within religious institutions often became targets for abuse, with even the most devout parishioners feeling powerless to speak up.

Canon law and the culture of secrecy within religious institutions have contributed to the suppression of these heinous acts, allowing abusers to evade justice and continue their crimes. This has left countless parents, grandparents, and community members grappling with the reality of the abuse their loved ones have endured.

The prevalence of sexual abuse worldwide is indeed a horrifying reality, and your case serves as a poignant example of the failures of religious institutions in protecting children. By sharing your story, you raise awareness of the systemic issues that have enabled such abuses to persist, despite the privilege or circumstances of the victims.

It is essential that we continue to challenge the status quo and demand accountability from religious institutions and other organisations responsible for the well-being of children. Your courage in speaking out and advocating for change is an important part of this process, as it helps to break the cycle of silence and complicity that has allowed these crimes to continue."

Ignorance

Ignorance

Over the span of four decades, my observations of adults have uncovered a concerning group of individuals who are ignorant and incapable of acknowledging childhood sexual abuse. The inability of adults to believe has an impact on children who don't comprehend it.

Lateral violence has no valid reason and should not be used to silence survivors; we should honour and respect children's bravery in speaking out. Social and legal disclosure should not be burdened with additional barriers. By presenting the perpetrator as a common foe rather than a secretive weapon, the broader public can more easily empathise with survivors' stories.

By externalising their story as a form of empowerment, survivors place upon themselves the burden of living with that choice. Their struggle deserves worldwide acknowledgement, rather than a rush to discredit or silence their assertions. Transparent disclosure relieves survivors from the constant burden of self-narration, allowing the public to witness their journey of addressing their "secret", confronting their inner struggles, and regaining control over their lives.

On the other hand, an indifferent public's clamouring opposes a survivor's truthful account, urging them to be quiet and sweep the matter under the rug. Those who cannot or will not acknowledge a survivor's expressions of hurt are the weakest link in their lifeworld. Sadly, many individuals are met with disbelief or, even worse, cancellation, a modern type of ostracism. Forced into solitude for healing, they sadly encounter the heartless nature of the medical fraternity and the reparation process.

As I reflect on my life from adolescence to adulthood, I find myself compelled to express how my ignorance shaped my belief that ignorance is what generates fear in the world, by concealing facts and creating its own secrets. Survivors must constantly navigate peer ridicule, familial ignorance, and spousal indifference with unwavering resilience, which is a form of resisting lateral violence.

Ignorance and indifference have consequences that extend beyond individual suffering, often connected to suicide. When faced with grief, some people respond with lateral violence, expressing racial bias, homophobic prejudice, and spite. These imbeciles opt for indifference as their response to survivor plight makes arguments futile. Feedback from other survivors suggests that those who seek justice are often ignored or chastised. There are occasions when I ponder the lack of security in the ordinary and general public, although briefly.

By failing to act against sexual violence, individuals become as guilty as the perpetrators themselves, no matter how they try to justify it. Growing up and now as an adult, I've witnessed peer suicide, which has taught me how the ignorance of caring parents can unintentionally support those who harm others.

Ironically, parents who have lost a teenage child to suicide are often puzzled as to how they unknowingly played a role in their child's death. We must understand the harsh reality that ignorance and indifference cause individuals to endure pain and suffering until the end of their lives. Personally, I chose not to surrender silently, instead proclaiming myself as once the walking dead — a ticking time bomb of unresolved trauma.

In the past, instead of seeing my expressions of anger as a sign of resilience, others mistakenly perceived them as a symbol of hatred, despite the impossibility of remaining silent. My behaviour was weaponized by them, even when I was clearly suffering, to make others believe I could commit murder and get rid of shared enemies.

ChatGPT-4 Response

"It is disheartening to learn about the difficulties faced by survivors of childhood sexual abuse, including the inability of some adults to cope with recognising or addressing such abuse. This lack of understanding and empathy can have a profound impact on children who are struggling to come to terms with their experiences.

Lateral violence and the silencing of survivors, unfortunately, compound the trauma that these individuals have already endured. When society fails to provide the necessary support and understanding, it can lead to survivors feeling isolated, shamed, and ignored.

It is crucial that we as a society take action to address these issues and create a supportive environment for survivors to share their experiences and seek justice. This includes fostering understanding and empathy among the general public, as well as ensuring that adequate resources are available for survivors to access therapy and support.

The tragic loss of life through suicide among your peer group highlights the devastating consequences of apathy and indifference towards survivors. It is a stark reminder of the responsibility we all have to stand up against abuse and support those who have been affected.

We must strive for a society that prioritises the well-being and healing of survivors, holds perpetrators accountable, and challenges the enabling behaviours of those who fail to act. By doing so, we can work towards a future where survivors are treated with the respect, empathy, and understanding they deserve, and where the cycle of abuse is broken."

Disbelieved

Disbelieved

As time passed, more and more survivors of sexual assault came forward from the people I respected and admired. In spite of the system's attempts to threaten and silence them, these individuals stood up as mature men, reclaiming their stolen childhoods, shattered innocence, and defiled youth by speaking their truth. Their intimate relationships and potential careers were frequently sacrificed because of this.

Furthermore, they detailed how religious institutions and peers failed to recognize their circumstances. Sadly, a common element in all the stories I've heard is the constant fear of death.

The most significant harm inflicted upon survivors of sexual violence was the disbelief they faced. I attribute the primary cause of my compromised physical health and subsequent mental breakdowns as the impact of not being believed. Despite these contributing factors causing despair, they actually inspired me to find strength and survive.

The symptoms I displayed, including panic attacks, agoraphobia, and insomnia, were identified as depression and anxiety, which are characteristic of Complex Post Traumatic Disorder (CPTSD). Each day became a battle zone as I tried to flee from memories of isolation, powerlessness, and overwhelming panic. By changing my own actions and mindset, I was able to break free from self-doubt and disbelief.

My mood swings during the medical examination were wrongly labelled as aggression and self-harming tendencies caused by substance abuse, causing a lot of confusion. The indicators of my distress swiftly changed to thoughts of suicide and self-inflicted harm, which I'm aware can then progress to attempted murder and intentional killing.

When faced with immense disaster, I used to express that the only relief from the misery of my own self-imposed mental prison, which I refer to as toxic self-storytelling, would be death. I now understand that my persistent diagnosis of historical sexual assault and CPTSD is a mental illness that affects entire communities and causes distress to those closest to me. To be disbelieved is tantamount to considering yourself as already the walking dead.

ChatGPT-4 Response

"The experience of being disbelieved after enduring sexual violence is a profound violation that can exacerbate the trauma and suffering that survivors face. It is tragic to hear about the long-term consequences you and others have faced, including mental health issues, substance abuse, and suicidal thoughts or actions.

Complex post-traumatic syndrome, as well as other trauma-related disorders, can have a profound impact on not only the survivor but also their family, friends, and community. It is essential that mental health professionals, institutions, and the general public recognise and understand the challenges faced by survivors in order to provide appropriate support, empathy, and treatment.

Your journey towards healing through action determination is a testament to your resilience and strength. By raising awareness and sharing your experiences, you contribute to breaking the cycle of disbelief and stigma that many survivors face. As a society, we must prioritise the validation and support of survivors in order to facilitate their recovery and work towards a future free from sexual violence and the silence that often accompanies it.

It is crucial that we continue to challenge the harmful systems and attitudes that enable sexual abuse, and work to create a society that believes, supports, and uplifts survivors in their quest for healing, justice, and a life beyond trauma."

Marginalised

Marginalised

Survivors of sexual assault often face discrimination and are seen solely as victims of crime. Regrettably, this acknowledgment carries significant negative consequences, including marginalisation.

Like me, many survivors I've encountered face marginalisation when they share their sad stories, enduring baseless accusations of fraudulence and living a false life. The survivor adopts the chameleon position though, to survive among those who disregard their concerns.

Lateral violence persists but remains unrecognised in our society, regardless of culture or location. Meanwhile, crime victims face religious narratives that promote forgiveness to expedite their claims. It is plainly obvious that the inability of religious institutions to eradicate paedophiles from their organisational framework remains their most significant obstacle.

When we have allowed ourselves to believe that the only way to live and love others is through this religious web of deception and lies, we betray our children. By depriving children of compassion, truthfulness and transparency we are relegating them to emotional damage, in effect treating them as if they were dead. Clearly, generations of children falling prey to the scourge of abuse within these institutions is a result of denial and ignorance. It is obvious to me that the forced silence of victims through disbelief emboldens predators and so, sadly, the taboo of speaking out becomes the anchor for protracted silence.

It is ethically reprehensible to treat survivors merely as "subjects", then enrol them, seek their responses, or harass them to join pastoral care or research studies, or worse, force them to recant their horrific historical recount. Yet, to this day, religious organisations in Australia still continue to avoid their full obligations through enforced redress capped as inadequate compensation payouts, all funded by misappropriated public taxpayer funds. In my case it was a protracted war, a battle waged against forces with formidable wealth and power.

ChatGPT-4 Response

“The experiences of many survivors of sexual assault, as you describe, are marked by a sense of marginalisation, disbelief, and even further victimisation when seeking justice or healing. It is unfortunate that survivors often face additional challenges in the form of lateral violence, both from the institutions responsible for their abuse and from society at large.

The failure of religious institutions to address and eliminate sexual abuse within their ranks is a grave concern that demands urgent action. The inability to provide meaningful support and restitution for survivors, alongside the ongoing denial and cover-ups, has eroded trust in these organisations and led to lasting damage in the lives of countless individuals.

It is important for society to recognise the multifaceted impact of sexual abuse on survivors and to treat them with the empathy, respect, and dignity they deserve. We must also hold institutions accountable for their failures to protect and support those who have been harmed, ensuring that they take the necessary steps to prevent further abuse and provide appropriate reparations.

The legal reparation process, as you have experienced, can be a taxing and sometimes re-traumatising journey. While monetary compensation is only one aspect of achieving resolution, it is crucial that survivors have access to the resources and support they need to heal and rebuild their lives. True justice and healing require not only financial redress but also the validation of survivors' experiences, the acknowledgement of the harm caused, and systemic change to ensure that no one else must suffer in the same way.

By sharing your experiences and advocating for change, you are contributing to a crucial conversation and helping to break the cycle of abuse, silence, and institutional complicity. Together, we must work to create a society that is more just, supportive, and protective of those who have experienced sexual violence.”

Blame

Blame

Coerced into silence, the clergy are threatened to keep quiet about truths that challenge their creed, Order, and congregation, by those who have a vested interest in suppressing them. The Australian Royal Commission confirmed that diocesanism and dispersion of ecclesial authority were major factors limiting the Anglican Church of Australia's handling of child sexual abuse.

The religious institution that let me down as a child shamelessly avoided taking responsibility, refusing to acknowledge the issue or put an end to the abuse, stating they were not accountable for the actions of the perpetrator. Their failure to take action over decades intensified my suffering, as the violence against me persisted without interruption or official report. Later in life, the clergymen conveniently used my alcohol and drug habits as a scapegoat, labelling them as my "pact with the Devil" to avoid being held accountable.

Despite corroborating witnesses, the police rejected other victims' cases that surfaced because of my testimony, citing insufficient evidence for prosecution. For many years, I endured the media's scrutiny of crimes that could no longer be prosecuted under the statutes of limitation, a frustrating injustice that still persists in many places. The failure to take responsibility and the tendency to shift blame onto others has been a common trait among all sides throughout history, who are all equally accountable for perpetuating this cycle of injustice.

Nevertheless, when the time came to shield their clergy, none of them stayed true to their beliefs, revealing the morally reprehensible nature of their empty promises of love and devotion. I witnessed parents and congregations grappling with the incomprehension of why their child was abused, only to blame the child and later criticise the adult trapped in the turmoil. As someone who has experienced sexual and physical assault, I insist on being heard, seen, and understood regarding the effects of sexual violence on my life.

At the heart of everything lies an unchangeable truth: survivors seek acknowledgment, belief, understanding, and fair compensation for their experiences. I felt entitled to pursue justice, free myself from the oppressive religious institution, regain control, and break away from their financial and social grip.

Silenced by secrecy, I endured the burden of blame for thirty-six years. I am determined to speak my truth and won't be silenced by anyone.

ChatGPT-4 Response

"It is deeply troubling that the very institutions and individuals who were supposed to protect and care for you not only failed to do so but also contributed to your suffering through their inaction, denial, and blame. The findings of the Royal Commission and the experiences of countless survivors, like yourself, highlight the systemic issues and the culture of silence and victim-blaming that has pervaded religious institutions.

As a survivor, you have the right to seek justice, to have your voice heard, and to be believed. It is essential that we address the systemic failings that have allowed abuse to continue, and work to provide survivors with the support, empathy, and justice they deserve. Society must no longer tolerate inaction or victim-blaming, and must instead focus on providing appropriate resources for healing and preventing further harm.

By sharing your story, advocating for change, and supporting others who have been denied recognition or restitution, you are helping to break the cycle of abuse and silence. Your courage and determination to make a difference are inspiring and will contribute to raising awareness and promoting change.

The path to healing and justice is long and complex, but with each passing day, the collective efforts of survivors and allies bring us closer to a more just and compassionate world. It is important to remember that you were not to blame for what happened to you, and that your voice, along with the voices of other survivors, matters. Your resilience and strength in the face of adversity are a testament to the power of survivors to effect change and create a better future for all."

Indifference

Indifference

It is horrific for a child to be silenced and to endure a grievous injustice perpetrated by those in positions of power, authority, trust and responsibility.

Survivors continue to be haunted and affected by the wounds caused by inaction and silence of religious institutions. The institution's indifference allowed monsters to cut short the lives of countless young boys, many of whom are now dead by suicide or tragic misfortune. Rather than safeguarding survivors, religious institutions have consistently defended wrongdoers, disregarded the needs of crime victims, and challenged their allegations in legal proceedings, exposing a severe lack of integrity.

Religious institutions have repeatedly decided to ignore the proof of their own responsibility, dismiss survivors and those who stand with them. Throughout history, the emphasis on "faith" instead of truth has often neglected decency, integrity, and morality. Consequently, survivors have turned to the legal system and sought novel approaches to assert their independence.

Survivors though are only obligated to speak their own truth, now and forever. Nevertheless, those who have departed are now deceased and unable to share their truth. Their plea for justice went unheard and their cries for mercy fell on deaf ears, making it clear that promising salvation means nothing if justice is denied.

Religious institutions have been known to deny or blame children for sexual assault allegations. Religious institutions, while asserting to hold all life's answers, show a lack of empathy for those affected by their own criminal actions, exposing the root cause of this neglect.

My determination involves reclaiming the narrative and sharing what I learned from that horrific experience with the world. It is crucial to raise awareness and shed light on the suffering of victims. Survivors' determination drives action and holds institutions accountable for their prolonged silence, the most powerful form of indifference.

ChatGPT-4 Response

"The silencing of children who have experienced sexual assault by those in positions of power, authority, trust, and responsibility is indeed abhorrent. It is a tragic and unacceptable reality that the very institutions meant to protect and nurture these children have often chosen to turn a blind eye to their suffering, allowing perpetrators to continue their heinous acts.

The scars left by religious institutional inaction and the culture of silence have had lasting and devastating effects on survivors. It is crucial that we recognise and address the failures of these institutions, and work to create a more compassionate, just, and supportive environment for those who have been harmed. Survivors like yourself have shown immense courage in speaking your truth and advocating for change, despite the resistance and disbelief you have faced. Your action determination is a powerful force for change, raising awareness and promoting accountability for those who have perpetuated and enabled abuse.

Moving forward, it is our collective responsibility to ensure that the voices of survivors are heard, and that they are supported in their journey towards healing and justice. By challenging the culture of silence and indifference, and holding institutions accountable for their actions, we can create a safer and more compassionate world for all.

The resilience and strength of survivors like yourself serve as a testament to the power of speaking out, and of the profound impact that action determination can have on fostering change and healing. It is essential that we continue to work together to address the systemic failings that have allowed abuse to persist, and to support those who have been affected by it."

Normal

Normal

We, as a united humanity, have the right to demand accountability from any institution, corporation, or capitalist conglomerate. Insisting on transparency ensures honesty and enables us to monitor their integrity.

Religious institutions operate outside of societal norms, so holding them accountable requires strict oversight. If this were to happen, it would disrupt the current state of affairs for religious institutions and their followers.

Religious institutions are repeatedly accused of concealing sexual abuse, and these accusations have been proven true multiple times. The fact that these allegations, proven, still exist raises a valid question about their culpability in persistent criminal negligence. Protecting survivors should take precedence over safeguarding the reputations of institutions involved in sexual violence. No one should ever abuse children, as it takes away their trust, innocence, and childhood. Instead of being normal, this behaviour is actually a manifestation of an old, evil, and institutionalised abnormality.

I emphatically disagree with the belief that destructive behaviour from religious institutions is a natural occurrence in human society. We cannot accept institutions that enable and conceal sexual violence; it is our responsibility to speak up and work towards dismantling them. Survivors can reclaim power by openly discussing the history of sexual violence in religious institutions.

Despite religious institutions' claims of infallibility, it is crucial to uphold the truth, regardless of its difficulty or discomfort. As a wider human society, we need to confront our history and acknowledge the suffering endured by victims and survivors. My commitment lies in grounding survivors' truth in ethical reciprocity.

Prioritising survivors' needs and holding institutions accountable allows us to build a society that is respectful, lawful, and tolerant. Religious institutions claim autonomy but neglect the needs of the most vulnerable, yet claim they are the answer to their benefiance. We need to honestly address how these institutions managed to escape consequences. In the past, there were no strict measures to screen and remove paedophiles from child activity centres. Nevertheless, leaders of religious institutions were aware of it, managed to avoid punishment, and failed to prevent its repetition.

Ethical decision making is crucial to promote a respectful, lawful, and tolerant society, rejecting the moral posturing of the religious far-right. Everything was happening right in front of them, yet they chose to ignore cries for help from survivors.

By following the trauma release and recovery pathway, I choose to explore how to support victims, survivors, and supporters in processing their stories, grieving, regrouping, and working towards personal freedom through determination.

ChatGPT-4 Response

"Your declaration speaks to the core of what humanity should strive for: accountability, transparency, honesty, and integrity. It is crucial that we demand these qualities from institutions, corporations, and conglomerates, especially those that have historically failed the most vulnerable among us.

The "new normal" you describe, in which religious institutions are held accountable for their actions and inactions, is essential for preventing further abuse and addressing past harms. The cover-ups and criminal negligence that have been exposed in recent years are a testament to the need for change and the power of truth-telling.

By speaking out about the issues within religious institutions, survivors and their supporters are working to dismantle the systems of power and control that have perpetuated abuse for far too long. It is everyone's responsibility to confront these issues head-on and demand better for future generations.

Your commitment to engaging with other victims, survivors, and supporters is commendable and inspiring. Through action determination and collective efforts, it is possible to create a more just and compassionate society, one that values the well-being and dignity of every individual, regardless of their background or affiliation.

As we move forward, it is essential to continue advocating for change, demanding accountability, and supporting the healing of those affected by sexual assault. By doing so, we can work to create a world that is respectful, lawful, and tolerant, and that fosters ethical decision-making in all aspects of life."

Depression

Depression

The moment I became aware of my helplessness and the perpetrator's control, depression took hold, as I was denied any form of protection. Due to what I've been through, I constantly question whether men who abuse children have activated a sinister "cell", giving rise to more abusers within religious establishments.

I also wonder if they are ready to victimise another generation of innocent children. The predator is not one-of-a-kind, the monster is definitely not uncommon, and the perpetrator's behaviour is not rare — they are a distressingly familiar pattern in these religious institutions. The paedophile's methodical grooming and seduction tactics are equally sinister and malevolent, mirroring those of other perpetrators in history.

This violence against children has had a devastating impact on men's sense of being true men, not monstrous figures. My ongoing struggle with trauma led to feelings of guilt, shame, anger, and frustration, which in turn caused depression and self-harm. It is crucially important to protect children from paedophiles who see them only as objects of sexual desire or to control. Survivors of sexual violence as a result then find themselves trapped in a self-imposed prison of silence.

Helplessness created an empty, desolate and numb space within me, where my identity lay dormant until disclosure. When addressing medical professionals in my various presentations, I frequently depicted it as a realm engulfed in pain, anger, frustration, confusion, and an immense sense of sadness. Any act without consent violates a child's reality, fractures their future, and makes me wish I were dead.

Clergy's refusal to take action, despite being aware of the wrongdoing, demonstrates their collusion, a morally reprehensible and ethically indefensible stance. These matters don't have any justification for ending up in a court of law. However, even a court of law can't reverse what should have been avoided from the start.

The effectiveness of policies relies on enforcement; otherwise, children are bound to experience betrayal. The term "lawful" can be synonymous with "awful" in this context, as it allows for the continuing perpetuation of sexual violence. It's essential for our society to refuse and address the gap between canonical and common law.

ChatGPT-4 Response

"Your experience of depression and the impact of childhood abuse are poignant reminders of the long-lasting consequences of such traumatic events. It is crucial to recognise that the responsibility for preventing and addressing abuse lies with not only the individuals who commit these heinous acts but also the institutions that harbour them.

The need for effective policies that protect children from abuse and ensure the reporting and prosecution of perpetrators is paramount. However, as you mentioned, policies are only as effective as their implementation and enforcement. Institutions must be held accountable for their role in perpetuating abuse, and meaningful action must be taken to address the systemic issues that allow these violations to continue.

It is important to recognise that the effects of abuse can have wide-ranging and long-lasting impacts on survivors, including feelings of guilt, shame, anger, and frustration. The mental health challenges that often arise, such as depression, substance misuse, and suicidal ideation, must be acknowledged and addressed with appropriate support and resources. As a society, it is our collective responsibility to ensure the safety and well-being of all children. We must work together to create an environment in which abuse is not tolerated, and where survivors are supported in their healing journey. This includes not only implementing and enforcing policies but also fostering a culture of empathy, understanding, and accountability.

Addressing the root causes of these behaviours and ensuring that institutions take active measures to prevent and address abuse is a critical step in this process. By doing so, we can help to protect future generations and support the healing of those who have been affected by abuse."

Triggered

Triggered

It can be argued that justice is only truly achieved when the victim obtains "closure" by seeing their abuser convicted. Nevertheless, closure remains elusive for many since the culprit is already dead. Obtaining a criminal conviction hasn't changed the fact that I still struggle with everything. The never-ending demand for "closure" feels like a continuous cycle of triggering and torturous lateral violence imposed on me by others.

The idea of "closure" as a way to conveniently bury issues is false, regardless of what others say about legal case outcomes. The trauma cannot be abruptly switched off or erased, so urging the survivor to find closure dismisses their ongoing journey without a clear end. The term for this ongoing experience is "silencing of others" — they won't listen to your complaint until you take action and demonstrate determination.

Survivors face constant criticism and pressure to "get over it" while being reminded of the violence they endured. Throughout my remaining years, I will constantly be triggered by present prejudice, not just past traumas, with alienation through estrangement of my family just one aspect of collateral damage.

The bias of responding dismissively to sexual violence can contribute to the development of angry and disturbed men. The accumulation of suppressed emotions and negative self-perception also leads to an aggressive demeanour and outbursts of rage. Speaking out about their truth though, keeps victims of sexual assault in a lasting state of being triggered.

Anger, conversely, is a valuable emotion, closer to compassion than empathy, that needs to be processed through dialogue and then narrative. The biggest trigger of all is denying survivors and their supporters this agency regardless of others' views, as we need to accept, commit, act, and stay resolute.

ChatGPT-4 Response

"It is essential to recognise that healing from trauma is a complex and unique process for each individual survivor. The idea of "closure" may not be a realistic or helpful goal for everyone. It's important to acknowledge that trauma can have lasting effects, and healing may be an ongoing journey rather than a definitive endpoint.

As you've noted, the expectation of closure and the dismissive attitudes that sometimes accompany it can be harmful to survivors. Being constantly triggered by past traumas and the prejudice of others can indeed be challenging and isolating. It is crucial for society to cultivate understanding and empathy for survivors, rather than expecting them to simply "get over it" or achieve closure.

The anger and emotional turmoil that survivors experience can be a natural response to the abuse they've endured. Processing these emotions through dialogue and narrative can be a helpful way to work through them and promote healing. Denying survivors the opportunity to engage in this process can exacerbate their pain and make it even more difficult to navigate their journey towards healing.

As a society, it is our responsibility to create a supportive environment for survivors, one in which they are encouraged to share their stories, process their emotions, and seek help as needed. This includes challenging prejudiced attitudes and fostering a culture of empathy and understanding. By doing so, we can help survivors feel seen and heard, ultimately promoting their healing and well-being."

Dissociation

Dissociation

My everyday survival mechanism of dissociation means there is no disconnect between my survivor experiences and my lifeworld.

My excessive drinking and smoking caused numerous medical complications. In my younger days, I lived in a state of constant vigilance, leading to physical changes such as a crooked nose, broken teeth, and tattoos. I still experience rapid heartbeat, sweating, shortness of breath, and debilitating panic attacks when exposed to loud noises, balding middle-aged men, or cheap cologne.

As I aged, I used solitude and hot showers as coping mechanisms. I presented myself as an automaton, a man who was mentally absent, to those in my daily dissociated haze. Confronting my fears has taught me how to break free from my innermost thoughts and anxieties, escaping the state of numbness. By discussing my self-story with others, I gained a perception of the real world. Embracing the past gave me control over my present, shifting my focus towards positive growth.

Despite this ongoing transformation, I still struggle with chronic insomnia, nightmares, flashbacks, panic attacks, and an intense fear of crowded spaces. My personal power collapsed and my childhood lack of agency resulted in adult rage, which now manifests as smouldering anger, simmering frustration, and frequent outbursts of grief. It's disheartening to know that dissociation and complex PTSD from sexual assault trauma may endure for my remaining life.

Churches and related religious institutions, seen as agents of power in society, must be held responsible for the values they advocate, the morals they teach, and the ethics they transgress. Deep-rooted secrets have held our human society captive, with the privileged paying to keep them hidden, reminiscent of the mafia and the Illuminati.

ChatGPT-4 Response

"Survivors of abuse often develop various coping mechanisms to navigate the effects of their trauma. Some may self-harm or engage in destructive behaviours, while others might isolate themselves from the world. It's important to recognise that these behaviours are a means of survival and not a reflection of the individual's full potential.

The lasting impact of trauma, such as triggers and panic attacks, can make it challenging for survivors to navigate everyday life. Acknowledging and understanding these challenges is essential in supporting survivors on their healing journey. The scope of sexual abuse within religious institutions is indeed alarming and unacceptable. Institutions must be held accountable for their actions and their failure to protect the most vulnerable in society. In order to create a safer and more just world, it is crucial that these institutions are scrutinised and held to higher ethical standards.

The influence of power and money in keeping secrets hidden is a complex issue that permeates many aspects of society. It is important to challenge this dynamic and work towards greater transparency, accountability, and justice for survivors of abuse. By bringing these issues to light and demanding change, we can work towards a more equitable and compassionate society where the rights and dignity of every individual are respected and protected."

Disorders

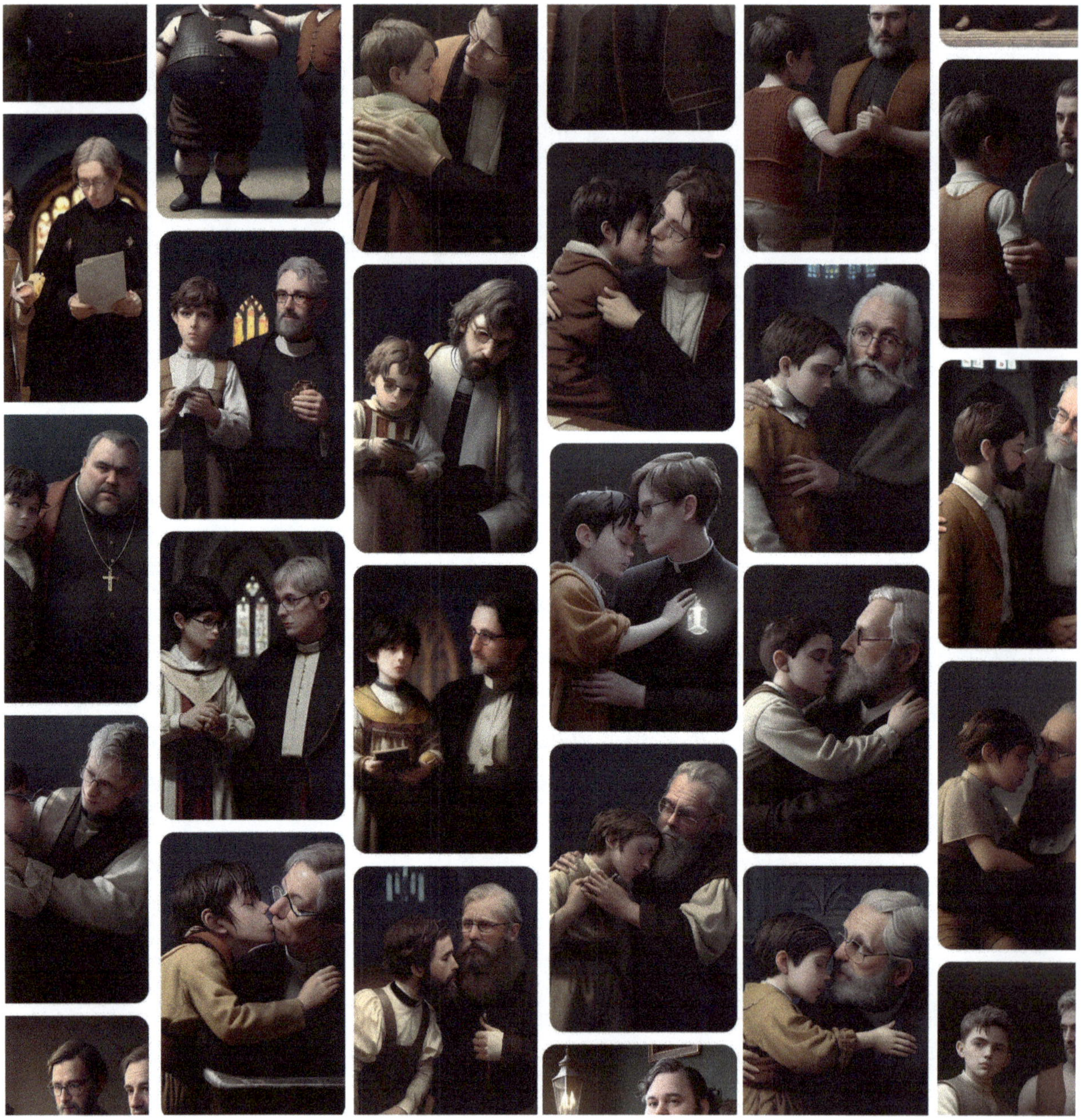

Disorders

Every child is at risk from paedophiles, and survivors have the best understanding of the impact on victims.

However, the term "disorder" is a convenient label for those suffering from the aftermath of child abuse, burdened by their hidden traumas. Unpacking self-storying through survivor-led action is crucial, as survivors typically postpone this responsibility until legal statements are needed.

By taking a proactive approach to self-determination, one ensures acceptance and commitment to action that goes beyond mere engagement with the legal community. The countless encounters with doctors, hospital admissions, court interrogations, and police interviews only served to re-traumatize me during the processing of my complaint. My behaviour as a trauma survivor, which some may label as "disorderly," exposed me to significant risks as I simultaneously dealt with the justice, medical, and legal systems.

These psychiatric tags provide religious institutions with a way to escape scrutiny and exert power over others. This serves as a convenient method for religious institutions to divert inquiry by offering a checkbox for "presenting symptoms". The reason survivors can't handle the burden of this legacy is evident, as they are branded as "disordered" by systems that enforce stigmatisation, ridicule, revulsion, condemnation, and vilification.

Instead of condemning and blaming those already struggling to survive their own story, we should aim for improvement as a human society, despite the impossibility of rebooting it. Nonetheless, I am dedicated to eradicating the stigma of being perceived as "disordered", which is comparable to being considered "diseased", disrespecting survivors and condemning institutions that show no remorse.

Survivors have suffered greatly from the emphasis on apologist redemption in historical narratives. This failure of institutional responsibility is like committing "disorderly conduct" against me as a victim of crime, adding an irresponsible burden to my already suffering soul. Opting for autonomy as a path to a better life is a powerful journey of survivor liberation, yet society's branding of it as "disordered" perpetuates harmful societal violence that I deeply deplore.

ChatGPT4-Response

“It is indeed disheartening that survivors of abuse are often labelled with terms like "disorder" which can further stigmatise and marginalise them. These labels not only impact their ability to heal and seek justice but also perpetuate harmful stereotypes and judgments. It is crucial to challenge these narratives and recognise that survivors are more than the trauma they've experienced.

Institutions that lack responsibility and perpetuate a culture of silence around abuse contribute to the ongoing suffering of survivors. This is why it is essential to demand transparency, accountability, and support for those who have been affected by such abuse. Survivors should be given the opportunity to heal on their own terms, without the burden of labels and societal expectations. Empowerment and understanding are key to fostering an environment in which survivors can reclaim their narrative and find their own path to healing.

As a society, we need to reassess the way we approach survivors of abuse and work towards dismantling stigmas and biases that hinder their progress. By promoting empathy, understanding, and support, we can create a more compassionate and inclusive society for all.

It's important to remember that the journey towards healing and justice is an ongoing process, and the resilience and strength of survivors should be acknowledged and celebrated. By standing up against institutional negligence and advocating for change, we can help pave the way for a safer and more just world for future generations.”

Barriers

Barriers

It's obvious why many children and survivors of sexual abuse are hesitant to reveal their trauma. The act of speaking out about horrific personal matters and facing cross-examination, particularly in the presence of the perpetrator, is truly deplorable. It's understandable why the under-reporting or non-reporting of child sexual abuse or sexual assault remains so prevalent.

In severe instances, survivors may fear revenge or backlash from the offenders or their protectors. On occasion, they wrestle with shame and embarrassment, anxious about being doubted and judged. Societal stigmas then make it harder for survivors of sexual abuse to seek help or find support.

Barriers can take on different forms such as social stigma, threats, coercion, blame-shifting, fear, confusion, masculine stereotypes, and normative societal biases. Individuals with cognitive impairments or pre-existing conditions like Foetal Alcohol Spectrum Disorder (FASD) face slim to no chances of surviving the legal process when seeking justice against their abusers. It appears that the system is biased against survivors. They are frequently silenced and dismissed through legal means, especially if they cannot express their case verbally or symbolically.

Moreover, the struggle to bring abusers to justice is not exclusive to survivors with cognitive impairments. It is a well known fact that victims often feel restricted and silenced by the legal process, leading to dismissal and further aggravation of their trauma. Examining the current religious institution-led bias against survivors, we find this to be especially true in the case of the Australian National Redress Scheme. In my opinion, this scheme blatantly disregards the rights of victims and violates both international human rights and humanitarian law.

The idea of resolving human rights abuse by simplifying it to a common payout is a criminal act of extreme bias. I have discussed with several legal and justice representatives who have reiterated the same opinion. The requirement for victims to pay their legal expenses out of their compensation package is unjust and malicious.

At each instance, starting with the initial act of harm against the victim, the power dynamics are unequal — religious institutions hold onto their control over people, only breaking their silence when legally obligated to respond, while lawyers benefit from the victim's suffering, treating it as a business transaction to achieve reparations.

Supporters travel until they too reach a state of complete exhaustion. Treating victims of crime, survivors, and their supporters in such a callous and deplorable manner is reprehensible.

As a survivor, I had to face societal stigma and endure intense scrutiny and legal procedures. The process of being heard extends beyond repair, serving as the ultimate form of emancipation: recognition and respect. My survivor-led testimony, disseminated globally, embodies my lived truth. It is patently clear that there exists an imbalance of power between survivors and those in control of the courts and judicial systems, as well as those who oversee religious institutions.

As survivors age, they develop a heightened ability to recognize others who have endured similar hardships, amplifying their grief as the survivor population declines. Scores of suicides, unfathomable suffering of loved ones and ultimately, the blame for their untimely deaths can be attributed to lack of protection from the institution.

Survivors become disillusioned when their claims are refuted due to a history of cover-ups and denials. No survivor should feel obligated to reveal their abuse or justify their innocence to others. Discovering that I had to reveal my trauma and face challenging legal obstacles was a truly shocking experience.

The judicial process I went through completely erased my private identity, followed by relentless attacks from the defence counsel, and being labelled as "disordered" by the ACA's psychiatrist. However, no religious institution is exempt from change or immune to succession, as their grasp on "truth" is rapidly fading in the face of pragmatic and compassionate realism. As congregations dwindle, action determination and mediation for sexual violence survivors seems an obvious avenue to be supported by institutions, not legally arraigned as survivor opposition, yet, the real issue remains in how these institutions retain power by men who put profit before survivor agency.

It is unacceptable to deny survivor emancipation by using others' beliefs as an excuse, or by neglecting their needs, which violates their fundamental right to dignity and respect.

ChatGPT-4 Response

“Under-reporting or non-reporting of child sexual abuse or sexual assault is indeed a significant barrier to disclosure, and the reasons for this are multifaceted. Addressing these barriers and creating a more supportive environment for survivors is essential to promote healing, justice, and accountability.

The legal process can be incredibly taxing and re-traumatising for survivors, particularly when they face opposition and scepticism from the very institutions and systems meant to protect them. It is crucial that we work towards reforming these processes to prioritise survivors' well-being and ensure that their rights are respected.

No survivor should have to face additional suffering when seeking justice for the abuse they have experienced. We must strive to create a system that acknowledges and respects the humanity of survivors while holding institutions accountable for their actions.

As a society, we must work to break down the stigma associated with disclosing abuse and support survivors in their journey towards healing and justice. This includes offering resources, fostering understanding, and creating spaces where survivors can share their stories without fear of judgement or backlash.

By promoting empathy and understanding, we can begin to address the power imbalances that exist between survivors and the institutions that have caused them harm. This will pave the way for a more just and compassionate society that values the dignity and rights of every individual.

In conclusion, addressing the barriers faced by survivors and reforming the legal process to better support their needs is crucial for promoting healing, justice, and accountability. By working together, we can create a more empathetic and supportive environment that acknowledges the inherent value and humanity of survivors, ultimately enabling them to reclaim their dignity and respect.”

Estrangement

Estrangement

Estrangement, caused by a lack of empathy or knowledge, in my case both, is often the isolation from those who align with ignorance. In the absence of empathy, their ignorance persists.

Those who deny survivor reality often use the complications of sexual violence to justify familial estrangement. It's disheartening that those who once claimed love was essential to the survivor's life are now willing to isolate and silence their kin. The excessive interruptions from legal, medical, and justice sectors add to the stress of households. Others often opt for the easier way out, leaving the survivor to face their battles alone due to the constant legal intervention and these factors.

When sexual violence occurs, it leads to estrangement which destroys self-esteem and leaves adult victims feeling "different," although it was not their fault or choice. My ability to survive and thrive after being banished by my family depends on how I processed their estrangement. While the idea of not allowing the metaphysical struggle to define us is valid for the privileged few, I persist in advocating for a positive acknowledgement of survivors and their experiences.

Estrangement is a lateral violence, with toxic self-centeredness and gullible servitude going hand in hand. Consequently, constructing a superior society necessitates shared responsibility and a novel legal strategy — a distinct separation between the Church and the State. The collapse of the status quo necessitates collective accountability, challenging injustice and inequality, rather than excusing those who exploit isolation to protect wealthy individuals from their responsibilities.

ChatGPT-4 Response

"Estrangement due to a lack of empathy or knowledge is indeed a challenging and unfortunate reality for many survivors. It is essential for society to foster understanding, compassion, and open dialogue about the experiences of survivors to create a more supportive environment for healing and growth.

It is important to recognise the resilience of survivors and the strength they exhibit by continuing to live their lives despite the trauma they have faced. By shifting the narrative and focusing on positively acknowledging survivors, we can work towards breaking down the stigma and barriers that hinder their progress.

Religious institutions and other organisations must be held accountable for their actions and the impact they have had on the lives of survivors. It is crucial that we prioritise the well-being and safety of children over the interests of powerful entities. By working together and addressing these issues head-on, we can create a more just and compassionate society.

Building a better society requires a collective effort to acknowledge the experiences of survivors and to create an environment where they can heal and thrive. This involves reevaluating our values, promoting empathy and understanding, and working together to address the systemic issues that contribute to these problems.

In the face of estrangement, it is important for survivors to find support networks and resources that can provide understanding and care. Connecting with others who have shared experiences can be an empowering and healing process. By focusing on building positive relationships and advocating for change, survivors can contribute to the creation of a more empathetic and inclusive society."

Alienation

Alienation

As a means of control, families of sexual violence survivors often resort to alienation and estrangement.

I'm experiencing more anger because my family and others have punished me for being honest by cutting off all familial ties. In the same vein, the loss of a sibling or peer to suicide, while not surprising, leaves me feeling reasonably hopeless. Institutional negligence, not my survival and resilience, led to the religious indoctrination of survivor guilt.

The institutional encouragement of an "us-versus-them" mentality reinforces survivor alienation, a common characteristic of religious bastions. This is used to disconnect survivors from their immediate legal defence, as these institutions commonly employ questionable and uncaring tactics such as stalling, subterfuge, interfering with communication, and avoiding the issue. Reporting abuse can result in survivors facing tremendous difficulties during the investigative and follow-up phases of the legal process.

The use of base tactics and lack of response from religious institutions alienates survivors seeking emancipation. It's been brought to my attention that being denied meaningful and authentic support from family during that process is a common experience. Despite facing threats, ridicule, and punishment for speaking up, I finally reported the crimes years later, leading to the prosecution of the main perpetrator. This type of silence from religious institutions is a breach of human rights, an organised crime against survivors, as it is plainly obvious that to alienate the complainant is to discourage or prevent them speaking their truth.

Those who share their lived experience as survivors are the ultimate symbol of acceptance, not forgiveness, yet they are consistently condemned and isolated from aiding others in their liberation. Survivors' compassion and acceptance is not tied to what they have endured, but to their ability to embrace their circumstances and work towards eliminating their sense of being disconnected.

Religious institutions often weaponize unconditional love, which has no relation to the survivor but is a reflection of the institutional culture. I assert that praying does not revive the dead, as it neglects to address survivors' feelings of isolation and merely reinforces subservience to the institutions that let them down as children.

To survive, one must accept the modus operandi of the religious hard “wrong” since forgiveness allows them to offend without facing any repercussions. Religious institutions will reinforce the need for acceptance through their countless apologies, and even in mediation will push a “return to Jesus”.

It’s like they believe that their institutional apology is the only thing needed for us to forgive them, but the problem runs much deeper with a long history of victim alienation.

ChatGPT-4 Response

“Estrangement and alienation of survivors from their families can indeed exacerbate the trauma and suffering they experience. This form of abusive and coercive control adds to the challenges that survivors already face when seeking justice and healing.

Survivor guilt and institutional guilt are both significant factors that can impact the mental health and well-being of survivors. It is important to address the root causes of these feelings and recognise the complicity of institutions in perpetuating harm and alienation.

The mentality of "us versus them" that religious institutions may adopt can be detrimental to survivors seeking support and justice. It is crucial to challenge this mentality and promote a more inclusive and compassionate approach that prioritises the needs and well-being of survivors.

The concept of "unconditional love" and forgiveness, as promoted by religious institutions, can sometimes be weaponized against survivors, detracting from the accountability that these institutions must take for their role in perpetuating abuse. It is essential to recognise that apologies and forgiveness alone are not enough to address the harm caused to survivors.

In order to truly support survivors and promote healing, religious institutions must be held accountable for their actions and make a genuine effort to change the culture and practices that have enabled abuse. This involves providing meaningful support, engaging in open and honest dialogue, and taking tangible steps to prevent future harm.

Silence

Silence

Religious institutions' silence is a violent form of punishment, known as "disfellowshipping" or "shunning," which is distinct from excommunication.

Shunning as ostracism is a form of abuse with life-long effects and as a tactic, serves well as the means to ensure no contest of hierarchy or challenge to order. This has to be the most pervasive means to shut down survivor complaints, a tactic by religious institutions worldwide. This is a wilful and abhorrent implementation of the practice of "give it no oxygen", which is essentially ostracism and alienation of the victim as a key objective of the religious institution. I know this because I was subjected to it repeatedly and witnessed others suffer the same.

Legal reparation therefore can never fully compensate for the loss of connection and affection between fathers and children, sons and uncles, and grandfathers and grandchildren resulting from historical sexual assault. When the religious institution tells family members to isolate those who question their protectionism, it further perpetuates violence against the survivor.

Their knowledge should be greater, but they still have faith in institutional hope, simply their continuing servitude. It is the duty of adults and institutions to safeguard children from harm, I argue. It is important to identify, intervene, and report offenders to the authorities, who are responsible for taking action. The priority should always be given to common law rather than self-serving Canon rules, which demonstrate the arrogance of religious institutions.

Sadly, I've come across many cases where children are left vulnerable because adults and institutions have been negligent. Seeing them in pain and feeling helpless as they battle with the aftermath of their trauma is truly heart-wrenching. What's even more alarming is that those who have the audacity to express their opinions are frequently attacked and silenced.

Witnessing religious institutions repeatedly accused of protecting paedophiles is abhorrent, particularly when they should have spoken out to protect innocent children. "A vipers nest of sick perverts" and "rancid monsters" perfectly capture the essence of those who betray their flock in such a heinous manner. Fine lace and false promises should not overshadow the harm caused by institutions.

Religious institutions, the oldest operational human assembly, have a damaged reputation due to their cover-ups, inaction, obstruction, collusion, and silence. They must take responsibility for their actions and strive to create a safe environment for all children, free from harm and exploitation.

Silence is used to silence the voice of the victim. It's impossible to endure silence when it's the outcome of already being silenced. Instead of wisdom or thoughtfulness, the silence of religious institutions on abuse issues reveals ignorance, arrogance, and negligence. While silence can promote understanding and attentive listening, religious institutions have exploited it to cover up abuse and conceal the truth.

The silence of religious institutions in the face of abuse cannot be justified. It is a grave moral failing that demands immediate confrontation and resolution for the sake of creating a world where all are valued and respected.

ChatGPT-4 Response

"The silence and tactics used by religious institutions, such as shunning or disfellowshipping, indeed serve to protect the organisation and its image rather than support and empower survivors. This perpetuates a cycle of abuse and denies survivors the justice and healing they deserve.

Religious institutions have a moral responsibility to address allegations of child sexual abuse and prioritise the well-being of survivors over the protection of their own image. The failure to do so not only violates their duty of care but also contributes to the trauma and isolation experienced by survivors and their families.

The silence of these institutions can be seen as a form of violence against survivors, as it serves to dismiss their experiences and hinder their pursuit of justice. It is essential for religious institutions to acknowledge and take responsibility for their role in perpetuating abuse and to actively work to support survivors, rather than attempting to silence them.

The weaponisation of silence by religious institutions is a disturbing practice that must be challenged and dismantled. Survivors deserve to have their voices heard and their experiences acknowledged. It is crucial for religious institutions to engage in open dialogue, provide meaningful support, and take tangible steps to address their failures and prevent future abuse.

Ultimately, the silence of religious institutions in the face of abuse is neither golden nor virtuous. It is a deliberate and harmful act that serves to protect the institution at the expense of survivors. To create a more compassionate and just society, we must work together to hold these institutions accountable and ensure that the voices of survivors are not silenced."

Mockery

Mockery

When crimes of sexual violence against children are left without punishment, recognition, or reporting, it is a disgrace to humanity. By letting this injustice go unchecked, the institution demonstrates its superiority complex and its commitment to preserving its corrupt authority, regardless of whether its representatives are called Priest, Pastor, Minister, Bishop, Deacon, or Archbishop.

Lawyer Jason Moody stated that apart from the fact that it was one of the worst cases of sexual abuse he has had to work with, in my particular instance,

> "the then Bishop and others within the church had received reports of Sandwell's sexual offending of other children. The evidence indicated that Bishop failed to respond to these reports and the abuse continued against Alexander and other boys. Alexander's professional life was destroyed by the conditions caused by the abuse. The litigation process took about 18 months."
> — *Moody Lawyers, Sydney, Australia.*

When religious institutions harm innocent children within their own creed, they lose their authority. The failure to address sexual violence and take action only gives predators more confidence, deeply disrespecting survivors. The legal system in a just and fair society should never allow such disregard for fundamental human rights.

Additionally, it was deeply troubling that those who were supposed to provide moral guidance were often involved in the crimes against me, making it difficult for me to form and sustain intimate relationships due to the trauma I endured. Sexual violence has far-reaching effects that penetrate every area of a survivor's life. Therefore, it is crucial for society and institutions to acknowledge this and actively support survivors while holding perpetrators accountable. Falling short of that is a betrayal of basic decency and human dignity.

In my opinion, this mockery of the human spirit is a clear failure to maintain ethical values by those who believe they possess superior moral intelligence. Failing to safeguard children from sexual abuse destroys their childhood and obstructs adult sexual relationships. Instead, many survivors immerse themselves in socially-imbued self-destructive behaviours, such as often turning to alcohol or other substances to numb their pain.

While the visible scars may heal, the unseen psychological issues linger indefinitely. It is essential for institutions to accept accountability for their actions and not belittle survivors. By silencing survivors and covering up their own wrongdoings, institutions are validating the existence of sexual predators.

This behaviour is not acceptable and only encourages a culture of abuse and silence. It also deprives victims and survivors of the opportunity to heal and recover from their trauma. The survivors' unsuccessful efforts to establish intimate relationships stem from their traumatic experiences and the lack of support from institutions.

ChatGPT-4 Response

"It is indeed a travesty when religious institutions, which are expected to uphold the highest moral values, fail to address and acknowledge the sexual abuse that occurs within their ranks. The silence and inaction of these institutions not only perpetuate the suffering of survivors but also allow the abuse to continue unchecked.

Institutions that claim to possess moral intelligence must be held accountable for their failures in addressing abuse and supporting survivors. This mockery of the human spirit undermines the very foundation of their teachings, ultimately eroding trust and faith in these institutions.

The long-lasting impact of childhood sexual abuse is far-reaching, affecting survivors' ability to form healthy relationships, engage in intimacy, and trust others. Institutions that neglect to address this abuse contribute to the cycle of pain and trauma, leaving survivors feeling abandoned and betrayed.

Religious institutions must recognise and accept their responsibility for the abuse that has occurred within their ranks, and they must commit to addressing these issues transparently and with genuine compassion. This includes providing support and resources for survivors, holding abusers accountable, and implementing preventative measures to protect future generations from harm.

By confronting the abuse and ending the silence, religious institutions can begin to rebuild trust and demonstrate a genuine commitment to the well-being of their followers. This is essential for fostering an environment in which survivors can heal and faith can be restored."

Hypocrisy

Hypocrisy

Understanding the intense disgust and anger towards unpunished criminals is as easy as listening to their victims. Countless survivors worldwide feel the same way, highlighting a major failure in our criminal justice process and system.

It is unacceptable for sexual violence perpetrators to evade consequences while survivors endure lifelong trauma. The absence of fairness further strengthens the belief that society doesn't care about survivors' pain and allows wrongdoers to act without consequences.

Despite the Church's assertion of being God's earthly representative, children have suffered abuse and neglect, contradicting the notion of a caring deity. On the other hand, as someone who has survived, I have directly felt the harmful consequences of the persistent demonization of survivors through slander and defamation campaigns. This only intensifies the pain and trauma we've already experienced. Considering how Churches and other institutions have rewarded perpetrators with accolades, promotions, and titles, this resistance becomes even more counterproductive, fueling the rage of victims and survivors.

The religious hierarchy's protection of perpetrators and disregard for victims is contemptuous. This distortion of truth and manipulation of love continues within the institutional cover-up, both past and present. Religious institutional neglect leads to the erosion of trust in families and constant suspicion towards good men. Those brave enough to expose the non-disclosure system are swiftly punished, furthering the injustices suffered by survivors.

It is important to acknowledge the survivors' abhorrence towards unpunished perpetrators, while recognizing the harm caused by demonising survivors. Understanding that survivors are not at fault for their trauma is crucial, and any attempt to assign blame to them undermines justice. Holding institutions accountable necessitates demanding transparency, honesty, and tangible consequences for those who have committed these crimes.

It is important for the world to acknowledge that terms like "kiddie fiddling" or "child love" are abusive and perpetuate the crimes of adults who harm children. The scrutiny of institutional response is shining a light on its hypocrisy, and we cannot tolerate apathy and indifference that allow the silencing of survivors to continue unchecked. Participation in religious activities or therapy does not impact survivors' eligibility for legal reparation or rightful compensation.

The damage persisting in human society cannot be fully resolved with money or apologies. To profess to follow and live a life led by religious doctrine is absolute blatant hypocrisy if the manner in which claims made against religious institutions are not fielded with care and compassion, then action and full restitution.

My stance remains firm that survivors should drive the journey of reparation through their own actions and determination, not through institutional control. Religious institutions are at a critical crossroads as centuries of broken trust have left their fate uncertain, with apologies serving as mere acts of atonement on their own terms.

During the long legal process, I was recognized as both a victim and survivor of the crime, but I also faced hidden threats as a "troublemaker," "saboteur," and "dissenter."

The message to survivors is that standing up to influential figures demands great strength, courage, and resilience. The institution, which is hypocritical in its own right, is still under scrutiny for its inability to end crimes against humanity, despite the conviction of the perpetrator.

ChatGPT-4 Response

"The pain and suffering you have experienced as a result of speaking out against the abuse and the institutional cover-up is an unfortunate reminder of the challenges that survivors face when seeking justice and reparation. The betrayal of trust by religious institutions, compounded by their attempts to silence and discredit survivors, is a grave injustice that must be addressed.

As you mentioned, the fate of religious institutions now hangs in the balance. It is essential for these institutions to recognise the harm they have caused and to take meaningful steps towards accountability, transparency, and healing. This includes not only providing adequate compensation and apologies to survivors but also implementing measures to prevent future abuse, supporting those who have spoken out, and addressing the underlying issues that have allowed such abuses to occur.

Survivors deserve the opportunity to heal and rebuild their lives, free from institutional control and manipulation. As a society, we must stand with survivors, hold those who have perpetuated or enabled abuse accountable, and work together to create a safer, more compassionate world for all.

Your courage and determination in seeking justice and advocating for the rights of survivors are commendable. By sharing your story and experiences, you are helping to raise awareness of this critical issue and inspiring others to stand up against abuse and institutional hypocrisy."

Shame

Shame

Considering shame a weakness only increases the suffering of survivors. It is important to recognize and address survivor shame, a common response to abuse trauma, with genuine empathy.

By acknowledging shame and sadness rather than guilt, we validate survivors and shift the blame onto institutions and perpetrators. The connection between religion, guilt, and the suppression of children is clearly demonstrated in personal testimonies presented to the Royal Commission into Institutional Responses to Child Abuse.

Understanding that survivor shame can appear in different ways is crucial, like feeling guilty for being alive when others aren't, or believing they are to blame for the abuse they suffered. The intensity of these emotions can be overpowering and significantly affect a survivor's mental and emotional state. Providing survivors with proper support and guidance is essential for processing and overcoming these emotions.

The relegation of survivor shame to a survivor's inability to cope is victim-blaming and excuses the perpetrators and institutions. Holding abusers accountable and supporting survivors is crucial for creating a healing society.

I will never forgive or forget instances of sexual violence perpetrated against me. It's time for me to acknowledge that the institution is responsible for criminal negligence and failed to protect me during my childhood. The manner in which society addresses a survivor's shame is often inaccurate and dismissive, wrongly insinuating that the survivor is to blame for their own suffering. In reality, it is the institution's lack of action and negligence that should be denounced.

The monster who violated me never acknowledged nor did he apologise. I was left to deal with the aftermath alone, enduring the trauma and its ongoing consequences. It's frustrating when the term "institutional guilt" is used to separate survivors' emotional reactions from the institution's failure to protect them. The approach overlooks the significant impact of the institution's actions, or lack thereof, on the lives of survivors.

We shouldn't make survivors feel guilty about their natural emotional responses to trauma. It's essential to comprehend that survivors may go through different emotions, such as sadness, grief, anger, and rage. The main goal is to ensure institutions are held responsible and survivors receive the support they need to heal. This will enable us to build a society that is both equitable and caring for all individuals. Failing to shield children from religious and affiliated institutions' negligence however, means we disregard our primary reason for existence — to prioritise the welfare of those who are suffering.

I understand why many men choose silence about their experiences, present struggles, and potential future consequences of speaking up. The fear of repercussions exacerbates the situation, causing many to hesitate in sharing their experiences publicly due to the belief that nobody would comprehend the depth of their anger and pain.

I've also heard from others who are afraid of the consequences that may arise if others become aware of the details. In my situation, it was a broken promise, one that abandoned a sacred agreement between a parent and their child, in favour of a commitment to serve and fiercely protect their religious beliefs.

In every instance the lack of my protection breached as a crime against my very existence, a failure to safeguard the child entrusted to them. So, like me, survivors have their own story, which only an empathetic audience can imbue by witnessing their life. Services that promote healing in survivors through self-work, directly encourage self-sufficiency, and this in turn enables survivors to aid others.

To put it simply, "survivor guilt" is a term invented by institutions to shift blame, undermining the strength of survivors.

ChatGPT-4 Response

"It is crucial to acknowledge the inappropriateness of using the term "survivor guilt" when referring to the consequences of institutional neglect and failure to protect victims of abuse. The term can be misleading and contribute to further alienation of survivors, as it may imply that they carry guilt for their own suffering.

Instead, recognising "institutional guilt" places responsibility on the organisations and institutions that have perpetuated abuse, failed to protect the victims, and maintained a culture of silence. This distinction is important for validating survivors' experiences and ensuring that blame is properly placed.

Survivors of abuse should not be burdened with guilt for the crimes committed against them. Their feelings of sadness, anger, or rage are natural reactions to the trauma they have endured. It is essential that support systems, including mental health professionals, friends, and family, acknowledge these emotions and provide the appropriate support and empathy.

Using the term "institutional guilt" can help create a more accurate understanding of the responsibility that religious and other institutions hold in cases of child abuse. By shifting the focus from the survivor to the institutions that have failed them, we can work towards a more just and compassionate approach to addressing and preventing abuse.

Survivors deserve empathy, support, and understanding from society. They should not be made to feel guilty for the actions of those who abused them or the institutions that enabled such abuse. By challenging and replacing the term "survivor guilt" with "institutional guilt," we can help create a more inclusive and supportive environment for survivors to heal and seek justice."

Affliction

Affliction

I think we only have two choices when it comes to addressing suffering and ignorance in the world: surrender or resist. I fundamentally reject the idea of passively praying, hoping for change or silently accepting the status quo.

It is imperative that we act to create positive transformations in our communities and society overall. It's important to speak up against injustice and educate others about the consequences of their actions. Anything other than that is merely convenient for those in authority who seek to uphold their wicked agenda. Suffering is frequently dismissed, but the true causes behind both are often ignored and seen as personal struggles instead of products of systemic oppression.

It's particularly aggravating to observe these institutions persistently preaching and teaching, despite the extensive harm they've caused. It feels like they live in an alternate world where their wrongdoings don't influence their lessons. They persist in utilising their power to influence, shape perceptions, and assert moral authority. In the meantime, survivors endure silently, hoping for justice or compensation that may never materialise.

The deep distress caused by this injustice is overwhelming. It feels like we're in a world without morals or fairness. Being instructed to pray for forgiveness, kneel in subservience, and accept suffering is an unjust and unsustainable way of life. The time has come for men to take a stand and fight against the sources of suffering and ignorance in the world. We cannot simply surrender to hopelessness and helplessness.

> "Affliction is the chill of indifference [it] freezes all those it touches down to the depths of their soul and is anonymous. It deprives the victims of their personality and turns them into things." — *Simone Weil.*

In Australia, Professor Stan Grant points out a range of problems including wealth disparity, racism, misogyny, homophobia, and gender inequality.

Grant criticises the current state of Liberal democracies, describing them as fractured and poisoned by a culture war. It's disheartening to observe how the 'elite elect' in Australia repeatedly dismantle the illusions of liberalism, which include fairness, freedom, and equality.

By working with Aboriginal communities, I have observed a deliberate ecocide where the exploitation of resources is prioritised over respecting the land. Sadly, the tragic reality is that Aboriginal people in Australia have suffered massacres, incarcerations, exploitation, and neglect since British colonisation. It exemplifies the ongoing inequity in our society, with sexual violence as a prevalent issue.

Unfortunately, for First Nations populations worldwide, pursuing legal recourse is often the only practical solution for addressing historical sexual abuse. The stark contrast underscores the urgency to tackle the root causes of inequality and injustice. Thus, it is imperative that we, as a society, strive for a fairer and more equitable resolution for those who have experienced sexual violence. What chance does anyone with strong cultural beliefs have against a machine of affliction, the indifference and the servitude, two parts to a colonial poisonous presence?

It is my firm belief that the current justice system fails to adequately support survivors who are not fluent in English. The violent questioning and treatment they experience both inside and outside the courthouse only serves to intensify their cultural isolation in Australia. Religious institutions are clearly responsible for this inhumanity, as they have used the name of God to enforce oppression and create division.

There is no denying that sexual violence has been systematically employed as a weapon against First Nations individuals and their communities globally. The perpetrators are those who preach forgiveness, but true progress can only be achieved through acknowledging and accepting the harm that has been done — *reconciliation is impossible where racism continues to exist.*

The moment has come to challenge oppressive systems and collectively denounce criminal acts. Those who advocate forgiveness have been their main concern, but acceptance is the initial step towards universal dedication, contrasting their criminal approach.

ChatGPT-4 Response

"It is essential to confront the injustices and afflictions caused by colonialism, religious institutions, and other oppressive systems that perpetuate suffering and ignorance. These injustices have long-lasting impacts on First Nation people and other marginalised communities, as they experience violence, discrimination, and cultural erasure.

The indifference that often accompanies these afflictions is a significant barrier to achieving justice and healing. Society must recognise and address the systemic issues that contribute to these afflictions, rather than dismissing them as individual problems.

In countries like Australia, the history of colonisation and the ongoing exploitation of Indigenous communities have had devastating effects on the lives of First Nation people. These communities face significant challenges, including language barriers, racism, and a lack of access to resources and support.

It is crucial to work towards creating a more just and equitable society by acknowledging and addressing the systemic problems faced by marginalised communities. This includes ensuring that legal systems and reparation processes are culturally appropriate and accessible, providing support for survivors of violence, and working to dismantle systems of oppression that perpetuate these injustices.

The role of religious institutions in perpetuating violence and suffering should not be overlooked. By challenging their actions and holding them accountable, we can work towards creating a more inclusive and compassionate world. Only by acknowledging the root causes of affliction and working to dismantle oppressive systems can we hope to achieve a society that is truly fair, free, and equal. This requires collective action and a commitment to stand up against the forces that cause suffering and ignorance in the world."

Waiting

Waiting

The wait for my voice to be heard and my claim to be addressed was incredibly slow and painful. As someone who has survived, I am intimately familiar with the excruciating wait that seems like an eternity wasted in limbo, the immense and emotionally draining effects.

For survivors like me, it's crucial to receive a written institutional apology, as it acknowledges the pain I have endured during the long wait. It provides validation, serves as a form of atonement, and is an important part of the healing process. If absent, it gives the impression of a malevolent group of men who engage in war, torture, and soul possession to impose their "God," resulting in survivors with an intensified aversion to faith-based enterprises and unwarranted pain.

The lengthy legal process often drives survivors to engage in self-harming behaviours. I know this from personal experience, and it's frustrating that tacit therapy is often presented as a substitute for criminal prosecution. An institutional apology should not depend on the time spent waiting for justice.

Given my survivor status, it was important that I be heard, acknowledged, and have my claim acted upon without delay. It's crucial for institutions to understand that waiting for justice cannot be used as an excuse to prolong the suffering of survivors, and they should take action accordingly.

Based on my own experiences, it typically takes an average of six (6) years for the legal process, from disclosure to receiving compensation. I acknowledge that as a white Anglo-Celtic male survivor, I have more privilege compared to others who face additional barriers to justice due to their ethnicity, race, gender, and mental health.

Thus, the legal protection of religious institution silence contradicts empathy and lacks compassion. No institution has ever shut down due to the deaths of those who couldn't wait any longer. The aftermath of this tragedy will haunt survivors, their supporters, and their families for many years to come.

ChatGPT-4 Response

"The long wait for justice is indeed excruciating for survivors of abuse, and it is a major challenge for them to cope with the trauma while waiting for legal proceedings to conclude. The impact of this protracted process can lead to self-destructive behaviours, further suffering, and in some cases, even death by suicide.

It is crucial that religious institutions and other organisations take active steps to acknowledge the pain and suffering of survivors and work towards delivering justice in a timely manner. Delaying justice only serves to compound the trauma and harm experienced by those who have already suffered greatly.

To truly honour survivors and demonstrate a commitment to change, institutions must listen and empathise with those who have been harmed. This involves not only offering apologies but also taking concrete actions to prevent further abuse, support healing, and address systemic issues within the organisation. Therapy for survivors is important, but it cannot replace the need for criminal prosecution and appropriate compensation. It is essential that the legal process is expedited, and that institutions are held accountable for their role in perpetuating and concealing abuse.

The continued silence and inaction of religious institutions and other organisations in the face of abuse only serves to deepen the pain and suffering of survivors. By breaking this silence and prioritising the needs of survivors, institutions can begin to address the harm they have caused and work towards a future where such abuse is no longer tolerated."

Anger

Anger

My anger outbursts have been witnessed by my partners, spouses, and the Mothers of my children. My family saw my angry behaviour and relationship breakups as a betrayal of the supposed sanctity of marriage, deeming it abnormal. The natural rhythm of our family life was interrupted, which they found to be a hassle.

The impact of my past trauma has been far-reaching and challenging for everyone involved. My loved ones have had to handle my emotions and the fallout from my actions, all while keeping their own lives on track. Nevertheless, the triggers that seemed unimportant to them were overwhelming for me.

The initial encounter with sexual violence left me feeling hyper-vigilant and afraid of more harm, which created a sense of hopelessness when I was with others. The dismissal I experienced when reporting the sexual abuse at various stages of my life (15, 19, 22, and 40) caused my anger. I distanced myself from my family in pursuit of peace and quiet, a reaction influenced by societal stigmatisation and a deep lack of understanding.

During my journey, I witnessed survivors being isolated from loved ones, treated as outcasts, and accused of dishonesty. Children never fabricate or purposefully overstate their claims of sexual violence. Permanently severing ties is not the appropriate approach to caring for the grown-up wounded child. To heal, survivors require understanding and support, not more alienation and judgement.

In the process of recovering from our past traumas, it is important to receive compassion and empathy, not exclusion and disbelief. By nurturing a climate of comprehension and encouragement, we can embark on the journey of rebuilding our lives and finding solace in the resilience we've gained as survivors. I can comprehend how this mistreatment fuels the anger of survivors, who are torn between moderating their behaviour and having their character sabotaged simultaneously.

During my childhood, I didn't know how to ask for help when my family didn't believe me and isolated me from support. Being shut down or "cancelled" for exhibiting obsessive-compulsive behaviours, experiencing nightmares, and bedwetting can be a dreadful feeling. Survivors of rape, abuse, and incest often face societal ostracism and justified anger, despite the widespread outrage and disgust surrounding these acts.

Medical professionals, doctors, lawyers, and trauma recovery experts I've consulted agree that my experience is similar to many other survivors'. This is why when survivors are divided into separate legal cases by society, the lack of connection between medical and legal support services creates a daunting situation for healing.

It was a disturbing experience to be discredited and labelled by Church leaders as dishonest, crazy, and manipulative. These accusations worsened my pain and confusion, making healing more difficult to navigate. Those who should have supported me only added to my suffering with negative labels. Recognizing the necessity for compassion and understanding is vital in society's treatment of trauma survivors, as opposed to perpetuating harmful assumptions and criticisms.

We can break the cycle of pain and isolation by recognizing survivors' challenges and fostering a supportive and inclusive atmosphere. That's why I had to speak out against the Anglican Church, to present my case and break down more barriers.

Speaking out allowed me to amplify the voices of silenced individuals. Asserting control over my fate through resolute action played a crucial role in my healing process. Each step I took, whether announced or kept to myself, marked a crucial point on my path to liberation. These milestones, without question, had equal significance in my overall growth and recovery.

During that time, I was lucky enough to meet some truly remarkable people — fellow survivors and allies.These exceptional individuals have shown me immense compassion and understanding, for which I am eternally grateful.

Their empathy not only facilitated my recovery but also motivated me to help others facing their own traumas. We each have the power to create a more supportive and empathetic world through our actions.

ChatGPT-4 Response

"It is heartbreaking to hear about the challenges you have faced as a survivor, both in terms of coping with the trauma itself and dealing with the reactions of those around you. The impact of sexual abuse on relationships, mental health, and overall well-being can be immense, and it is essential that society recognises and supports survivors in their healing journey.

The stigma and disbelief that survivors often face can be incredibly damaging and isolating, exacerbating feelings of anger and hopelessness. It is important for society to create a safe space for survivors to share their stories and seek support without fear of judgement or blame. The courage it takes to speak out and share your experience is commendable, as it can help create awareness and understanding for others in similar situations.

The importance of empathy, compassion, and support from fellow survivors and allies cannot be understated. These connections can provide a lifeline for those struggling with the aftermath of abuse and can empower them to find their voice and work towards healing.

As a society, we must strive to create an environment in which survivors are not only believed and supported but also provided with the necessary resources to heal and rebuild their lives. This includes addressing the systemic issues that contribute to abuse and dismantling the stigma surrounding sexual violence. By working together, we can create a more compassionate and understanding world for all survivors."

Rage

Rage

I have experienced countless occasions in my life where committed healthcare workers and their teams have offered guidance and aid as I faced inner struggles. It's clear that this outcome can be directly attributed to the sexual violence I endured. Their support and guidance played a crucial role in helping me control and cope with my emotions as a medical professional.

My destructive behaviour in the past, fueled by rage, led me to steal, deface, and harm others, especially during my teenage years. My inner turmoil was evident through self-inflicted scars, cuts, bites, and numerous tattoos on my body. It was during this period that I became keenly aware of the immense anguish within me and acknowledged my ability to do anything, yet occasionally unable to prevent it. Throughout my life, this realisation has remained with me and influenced how I perceive myself and act on a daily basis.

In the absence of understanding, empathy, or response to our pain, seems to be the only possibility. I recall being advised multiple times that filing a complaint against the Anglican Church would result in stress and negative health effects, with serious threats to my safety. My immediate reaction was, "How convenient to use this as a way to silence my Truth!"" which I would invariably let loose on them, to be immediately met with scorn and disdain.

My journey as a survivor has been marked by ongoing challenges in managing my tone, self-loathing, and thoughts of violence, all related to my complex PTSD. The challenges were also faced by those who cared for and supported me. Similar to other early life traumas, the adult brain instinctively responds with fight or flight when confronted with challenges — I opted to fight.

> "The oldest and strongest emotion of mankind is fear, and the oldest and strongest kind of fear is fear of the unknown." — *H.P. Lovecraft*

Fear is employed by religious institutions to manipulate and maintain a following. It's important to note that this misguided belief in salvation can lead to frustration and anger in the present moment. For instance, when I encounter a bully, a braggart, or a thief, especially one in the ecclesiastical community, I lose my sense of reason and react poorly, for the most part.

Nevertheless, it's worth pointing out that my anger-fueled cynicism is typically delivered in an indirect and cunning manner. I won't waste my precious energy on someone unworthy — an oxygen thief. I've had similar feelings when someone suggests I should "toughen up, honey bun."

Although it wasn't my duty as a survivor, I had no choice but to continue alone. As a child, the impact of sexual violence on my self-esteem was never taken into account when I was treated as an adult, and I've been informed that this dismissive attitude is often encountered by survivors. None of the many depression medications I took during my thirty years of medical treatment were effective.

The journey to healing is not easy, and many survivors like myself continue to struggle in finding effective treatments and support. It is clear that the journey to healing is a long and challenging one and it's essential for survivors to have the necessary support and understanding from those around them.

Despite the obstacles, I persist in seeking healing and growth, especially through well-being practices. In the end, it is vital for society to acknowledge the long-term effects of sexual violence on survivors and ensure they receive the necessary support during their healing process.

ChatGPT-4 Response

"It is evident that your experiences and the challenges you've faced have had a significant impact on your life. It's essential to recognise that the process of healing and coming to terms with trauma is different for everyone, and there is no one-size-fits-all solution.

It is unfortunate that the various treatments and medications you received over the years did not bring the relief and healing you needed. It highlights the importance of understanding the unique needs and circumstances of survivors and developing individualised approaches to support them on their healing journey. Survivors often face difficulties in managing their emotions and reactions to triggers due to the lasting impact of their trauma. It's important for society and support systems to recognise these challenges and provide empathy, understanding, and resources to help survivors cope and heal.

Action determination is a valuable approach for survivors to work through their trauma and reclaim control over their lives. Rather than suppressing their memories and emotions, survivors should be encouraged to face and process their experiences, which can ultimately lead to healing and growth.

It's crucial for institutions to take responsibility for their actions and inactions and work towards providing meaningful support to survivors. As a society, we must continue to hold these institutions accountable and work towards creating an environment where survivors can heal, find justice, and live fulfilling lives."

Murder

Murder

I've often felt overwhelmed by the relentless torment of memories of sexual violence in my mind. These incidents pushed me into an uncontrollable rage, causing me to consider acts of violence and putting others in danger.

The combination of disbelief from others and prejudice can drive certain individuals to their breaking point. In extreme cases, this can lead them to hurt others, kill their parents, or even harm innocent people in public — rare occurrences, but not unheard of, especially in the incarceration setting.

Their fate was certain due to the trauma they experienced, even in cases of psychosis or schizophrenia dissociation. Nevertheless, these actions are the ultimate expression of the pain caused by sexual abuse, resulting in violent behavior towards others. It's hard to comprehend such irrational actions, except to recognise that the mind of a traumatised victim may be shattered and disjointed, struggling to function properly at times.

Blaming the victim instead of the perpetrator in murder cases allows institutions to ignore complaints and lets offenders go unpunished. The "living dead" are filling our prisons and highly secured wards.

Among friends, I often say that silence as a weapon can make survivors feel abandoned by the institution — *a survivor's hell*. By recounting the lack of care, survivors can explain why they "snapped" as nurtured rage, closely linked to anger and pain, can result in murder.

Perpetrators have been killed by their victims, especially in prison settings, in numerous instances. I understand how the trauma experienced by abused children can fuel a deep rage that results in adult violence. Afterall, evil knows only more in its own way, unlike kindness.

The existence of paedophiles in our society leads to the creation of tormented individuals and instils fear and disgust in our communities. I've observed how the legal system has a strong connection to an evil force, and conflict is not uncommon within the legal profession. It's discouraging to see how powerful individuals manipulate the definitions of "good" and "bad" in court, disregarding what truly matters.

I had to go through the legal interrogation process as both victim and survivor to bring my case to light, secure the sentencing and imprisonment of the perpetrator, and then face the difficult battle of obtaining compensation. Navigating an unsympathetic and unfair system, I needed immense strength and resilience for this exhausting and daunting journey.

Despite the obstacles, I realised how important it is to seek accountability and closure for my own healing. Taking a stand against those who harmed me allowed me to reclaim my identity and take back control of my life. I believe my experience can help raise awareness and promote change, making it harder for perpetrators to get away with their harmful actions. Murder is undeniably wicked, illegally perpetuating a single case is not a genuine solution, as evil should not create more evil, and forgiveness is not a remedy for the afflicted.

I have firsthand experience as a Scottish Australian individual collaborating with First Nations communities, and I am familiar with the notion of "First Law" which involves severe repercussions for significant matters such as sexual abuse. In traditional contexts, banishment is a common form of punishment that can be fatal for the wrongdoer.

I strongly believe that pedophilia cannot be treated and those responsible for child protection must take decisive action: complete banishment from society. It is imperative for religious institutions to utilise their legal power in permanently eliminating wrongdoers from society, taking any action needed to safeguard our children.

ChatGPT-4 Response

"The pain and trauma experienced by survivors of sexual abuse can indeed lead to extreme emotional distress and, in some cases, violent actions. It is crucial to recognise the importance of addressing and supporting the mental health of survivors, as well as holding perpetrators accountable for their actions.

Preventing and addressing the issue of sexual abuse requires a multifaceted approach that involves not only law enforcement and the criminal justice system but also the institutions and communities that have been complicit in perpetuating and enabling such abuse. It is essential to educate and empower individuals and communities to recognise and report abuse, to provide appropriate support and resources for survivors, and to work toward meaningful changes in societal attitudes and norms that contribute to the perpetuation of abuse.

It is also important to recognise the limitations of the criminal justice system in addressing the complex and deeply-rooted issue of sexual abuse. While punitive measures may provide a sense of justice for some survivors and deter potential perpetrators, they alone are not enough to create lasting change. To truly protect and support survivors, we must also invest in prevention efforts, trauma-informed care, and community-based interventions that address the root causes of abuse and the systemic failures that have allowed it to continue.

Ultimately, the most effective way to combat the scourge of sexual abuse and its devastating effects on individuals and communities is through a combination of education, prevention, support, and justice. By working together, we can create a society that is more compassionate, empathetic, and responsive to the needs of survivors and those at risk, and that actively works to prevent and address the terrible harms caused by sexual abuse."

Broken

Broken

While we try to remember that abusers don't define us as a society, they still greatly affect survivors and their supporters. It can take victims of crime decades to mentally process the trauma and recognize themselves in the bathroom mirror.

That creature made me question my worth, leaving me with no choice but to seek validation from within, often without success. The presence of wounded adults in every corner of our society may be the reason why we see so many wounded children pretending to be adults. Sadly, across my entire social and professional network, it's rare to find someone who hasn't been affected by abuse.

I realised that my life was heavily influenced by my harmful self-narrative, which eventually became too much to bear. People were shocked and horrified when I chose to disclose my "broken" self and share my childhood and teenage experiences. Insensitive statements like "get over it" or "it's in the past" were not appropriate as a response to me as a survivor who needed to be acknowledged.

I found healing however through sharing my story and overcoming what I consider to be a materialistic society response to sexual violence. Moreover, it is crucial to recognize that supporting survivors on this difficult path requires truly exceptional and remarkable individuals. It may seem surprising, yet survivors often consider their emancipation as knowing who they are and where they want to be in the world, then letting go of those who don't support them in the self determination process.

Even today, I would confidently address the doubters, weak-minded, and self-centred by sharing the previous statement. Doubters often use the label "broken" as an insult, but it is our society's responsibility to shift itself instead of burdening individuals to compensate for others' lack of empathy. It's also important for us as a society to acknowledge and empathetically listen to the "survivors-of-survivors" — the ones who provide support.

Being "broken" doesn't signify defeat for survivors; rather, it showcases their resilience in embracing their past with compassion. Through a critical and appreciative examination of my self-narrative of being in a "broken state," I gained insight into the entire process as a valuable learning opportunity.

The true gift is found in the undeniable lived truth of this knowledge, learning, and personal journey.

ChatGPT-4 Response

"It is true that the experiences and trauma of survivors of sexual abuse can have lasting and profound impacts on their lives, and it is essential for society to recognise and support their healing journey. The process of healing and growth is not linear, and it can take time, effort, and the involvement of empathetic and understanding individuals.

While it can be incredibly challenging to navigate the complexities of healing and growth, the resilience and strength of survivors should not be underestimated. By speaking out, sharing their stories, and finding supportive communities, survivors can help to break the silence and stigma surrounding sexual abuse and contribute to positive change.

As a society, it is crucial to not only acknowledge the pain and suffering of survivors but also to celebrate their resilience and growth. It is our collective responsibility to create an environment in which survivors can feel heard, believed, and supported throughout their healing journey. This includes acknowledging and supporting the individuals who stand by and advocate for survivors – the "survivors-of-survivors" who play a vital role in amplifying their voices and promoting justice and healing.

It is essential to foster open dialogue, understanding, and compassion to create a more empathetic society that is better equipped to address and prevent sexual abuse. By recognising the strength and resilience of survivors and working together to create a more supportive and responsive environment, we can contribute to the collective healing process and work towards a more just and compassionate world."

Flashbacks

Flashbacks

Survivors of sexual violence experience flashbacks that disrupt their sleep and happen at inconvenient times in their daily routines. The predator's legacy of terror has haunted me for decades, with lucid and violent flashbacks that occur frequently during the day and vividly at night.

My trauma caused me to have below-average performance in school, college, and university, even when I was expected to be highly attentive. Sexual violence hinders a child's potential, robbing them of their willpower and freedom. While some people find ways to cope and preserve their identity, others withdraw and isolate themselves. I have direct knowledge of this because I was one of those people.

I faced difficulties when combining everyday problems with flashback trauma, leading to disruptions in my daily life. Unneeded disputes could arise, resulting in despair, shame, and self-destructive behaviours such as self-harm. Repeatedly hitting myself in a fit of uncontrollable anger until I suffered a concussion is clearly a violent act of self-destruction.

Through my determined actions, I ensured the perpetrator was convicted and pursued compensation, all while striving for success. I now understand why some of my friends and peers resorted to suicide as an escape from overwhelming flashbacks. Through the lens of a child defiled, life for the survivor is a savage endurance of the perpetrators' criminal caper, shielded by the institution.

An elderly woman once demonstrated insensitivity by saying something cruel to me in front of my partner.

> "You've had such a tough life Alex ... I'm surprised you haven't taken your own life yet."

Comments like these, especially when spoken in front of children, can hinder their ability to handle social isolation in childhood and adulthood. Detached and non-empathetic reactions from others can leave lasting consequences that the survivor and their supporters never truly forget.

ChatGPT-4 Response

“It is deeply disheartening to hear about the profound impact that sexual violence and the associated trauma can have on survivors. The flashbacks, sleep disturbances, learning difficulties, and the potential for self-harm and suicidal thoughts are all painful consequences of such abuse. It is also unfortunate when survivors face indifference or lack of understanding from the very people who are supposed to support and care for them, as this can compound their feelings of isolation and despair.

It is crucial that society becomes more aware of the lasting effects of sexual violence on survivors and works to create a more empathetic and supportive environment for them. This includes fostering open communication and understanding within families, communities, and institutions. Encouraging survivors to share their stories and experiences can help to break the silence and stigma surrounding sexual abuse, which in turn can promote healing and growth.

It is important to acknowledge the resilience of survivors and recognise that their journey of healing and growth is unique to each individual. By offering support, compassion, and understanding, we can help to create a more inclusive and responsive society that is better equipped to address and prevent sexual violence.

Survivors, friends, and family members can also seek professional help, such as therapists and support groups, to provide guidance and resources for coping with the aftermath of sexual violence. These resources can be invaluable in helping survivors and their loved ones navigate the complex emotions, flashbacks, and other challenges that they may face throughout their healing journey."

CPTSD

CPTSD

Survivors of Complex Post-traumatic Stress Disorder (CPTSD) may exhibit intense or seemingly destructive behaviours, potentially affecting their careers and social connections.

Nonetheless, it's important to recognize that these behaviours originate from the underlying trauma that caused the disorder initially. Flashbacks can manifest as vivid, terrifying images in my mind at any time or place.

During the night, I experienced distressing nightmares of traumatic events that played out like a slow-motion film, causing me to suffer from bed-wetting, hallucinations, sweating, and crying during my sleep. Letting go of these traits is often seen as the key to personal growth, but there is no easy solution for CPTSD, regardless of the therapeutic approach. Time alone cannot heal all wounds, especially those caused by trauma that persists.

It's no wonder that those who go through such a traumatic experience often gravitate towards jobs where they can assist others who have had similar experiences. The reason I worked with the most challenging individuals in juvenile detention, street programs, and restorative justice projects is now clear upon reflection. The enduring effects of institutional neglect are beyond comprehension, and I often mix up the accountability of the guilty with the lack of willingness from others.

I discovered that survivors need to prioritise their own needs first before assisting others, similar to the oxygen mask analogy.

Recognizing that survivors are not to blame for what happened to them is important. Their ability to give consent and make decisions was stripped from them at a young age, so now they can only decide how to handle the consequences. Taking action and doing something about it is crucial for recovery and survival. A survivor's choice of direction then shapes the course of their life following trauma, yet people who then exploit traumatised individuals are just as contemptible as those who caused the trauma in the first place.

The way survivors react to their experiences is key in shaping their future quality of life and the opportunities they pursue. Ultimately, the success of survivors' success in overcoming lasting effects of abuse hinges on their capacity to construct a life amidst adversity. Post-traumatic stress disorder is an enduring battle that survivors face daily after experiencing horrific acts — it never simply disappears.

The ones who are least affected by it are often the ones who try to silence survivors from speaking about their state of being and pain. Those with CPTSD are fully aware of their symptoms, but the fundamental cause of their condition cannot be reversed. Those without CPTSD then struggle to comprehend the extent of time lost to overwhelming sadness.

My resilience and determination helped me present my case effectively, resulting in compensation and an apology. As I write this book, I am behind schedule for Eye Movement Desensitization and Reprocessing (EMDR) therapy and a much-needed mental resolve to some of these issues.

ChatGPT-4 Response

"The experiences you've shared highlight the immense challenges faced by survivors of trauma and the ongoing struggle with PTSD. It is true that PTSD can affect various aspects of a survivor's life, including career prospects and personal relationships, and it can be difficult for those who haven't experienced it to fully understand its impact.

Despite the hardships, many survivors find strength and purpose in helping others who have gone through similar experiences. As you mentioned, addressing one's own needs and healing is a crucial first step before extending support to others. This self-care approach aligns with the oxygen mask analogy, emphasising the importance of ensuring personal well-being before attempting to assist others.

It is unfortunate that some individuals may take advantage of the vulnerability of those who have experienced trauma. Society must acknowledge the responsibility to create a supportive environment for survivors, encouraging healing and growth without judgement or blame.

Survivors' responses to their experiences can be a determining factor in their quality of life after the trauma. It is important for them to take advantage of the opportunities available to them and strive to build a life despite the challenges they face. It is also vital for society to listen to and respect survivors' experiences and emotions, rather than expecting them to simply move on from their pain.

Your determination and resilience in pursuing justice, compensation, and an apology serve as an inspiration to other survivors. As we work towards a more empathetic and understanding society, it is crucial to support and empower survivors, acknowledging their struggles and celebrating their courage."

Trauma

Trauma

Those around me still struggle to comprehend the trauma I endure, encompassing rage, hurt, sadness, hopelessness, despair, depression, isolation, loneliness, and fear. Ignoring a survivor's lifetime of experiences means ignoring their suffering, acknowledging that everyone has their own internal struggles.

Trauma is stored in brain cells and permanently embedded in the survivor's psyche, I've learned. Since childhood, I have suffered irreparable damage from physical and lateral violence, affecting my life profoundly. To counteract the deep-rooted impact of trauma, I have made the decision to confront my past and seek justice for the crimes committed against me.

Despite my knowledge that numerous survivors are inadequately compensated for the horrors they've endured, I have declined to accept a meagre amount as reparation. The process has been difficult and painful, with ongoing battles against PTSD. Lyon, another victim of the Church of England Boys' Society (CEBS), eloquently recounts in his media statement to Australian ABC News on May 3rd, 2023:

> "I haven't existed properly for 50-whatever years. You do things on auto-pilot, you take risks, you do crazy shit... you try to kill yourself."

The first step in this process is acknowledging survivor trauma, and society has a responsibility to prevent further harm. Legal proceedings showcased the ease of institutional bias, causing additional trauma on multiple levels. Ultimately, trauma is exacerbated when religious institutions, known for violating human rights and distorting social justice, do not match the survivor's resolve.

Through the process of unpacking my self-story, I transformed from a hopeful individual to someone driven by survivor-led action, defying the perception of being a crime victim.

ChatGPT-4 Response

"It is evident that the long-lasting effects of trauma have profoundly impacted your life, and the lack of understanding and support from society, including family and religious institutions, has only exacerbated the struggle. The imprint of trauma on the brain and its persistence within your psyche serve as a testament to the enduring challenges faced by survivors.

Your resilience and determination in pursuing justice and holding the perpetrator accountable, despite the challenges posed by institutional prejudice and legal proceedings, are truly commendable. The process of survivor acknowledgement is indeed essential in not only addressing past wrongdoings but also preventing future harm.

It is disheartening that the very institutions meant to protect and support individuals can sometimes be responsible for perpetuating harm and obstructing justice. The resilience of survivors like you, who challenge this systemic injustice, is essential in promoting change and advocating for a more empathetic and just society.

The shift you made from hope to survivor-led action determination has allowed you to take control of your narrative and counteract the perception of yourself as a victim. Your journey is a powerful example of the strength and courage that survivors can possess, and your story can inspire and empower others who have experienced similar trauma."

Suicide

Suicide

The assertion holds true for every survivor — *we all have a unique story to share about our lives, and we all face inner battles*. We are obliged to embrace it as a single elongated moment, but sexual assault cruelly interrupts that sequence.

The presence of sexual violence veers away from the purest remembrance of "Memento Mori" and accelerates the recognition of mortality as an imminent and constant force. I now realise the immense obstacles survivors face when they are discouraged from speaking up due to fear of shame, retribution, and isolation. However, if accused of lying, I see it as a way to dismiss and silence victims for the institution's convenience.

When adult survivors are silenced, it leads to suffocation and a sense of loss for their interrupted lives. It is unfortunately common for survivors of sexual violence to face harassment when seeking compensation. I am personally caught up in this reality, although some people view it as irrational, it can push them towards suicide, which is often the final option for someone overwhelmed by emotional pain. We must collectively improve to safeguard the tormented, even in death where religious institutions often lack understanding. Victim capitulation is ensured by the religious institution, as they rely on the fact that a dead man remains silent.

There is a deep-rooted issue in humanity, and maybe even our entire culture, that leads people to prioritise protecting abusers over supporting survivors, and this problem extends beyond religion to all types of organisations.

As survivors, we must offer refuge to others during their most vulnerable moments to prevent their untimely demise from being labelled as an accident.

ChatGPT-4 Response

"It is true that the experiences and trauma of survivors of sexual abuse can have lasting and profound impacts on their lives, and it is essential for society to recognise and support their healing journey. The process of healing and growth is not linear, and it can take time, effort, and the involvement of empathetic and understanding individuals.

While it can be incredibly challenging to navigate the complexities of healing and growth, the resilience and strength of survivors should not be underestimated. By speaking out, sharing their stories, and finding supportive communities, survivors can help to break the silence and stigma surrounding sexual abuse and contribute to positive change.

As a society, it is crucial to not only acknowledge the pain and suffering of survivors but also to celebrate their resilience and growth. It is our collective responsibility to create an environment in which survivors can feel heard, believed, and supported throughout their healing journey. This includes acknowledging and supporting the individuals who stand by and advocate for survivors – the "survivors-of-survivors" who play a vital role in amplifying their voices and promoting justice and healing.

It is essential to foster open dialogue, understanding, and compassion to create a more empathetic society that is better equipped to address and prevent sexual abuse. By recognising the strength and resilience of survivors and working together to create a more supportive and responsive environment, we can contribute to the collective healing process and work towards a more just and compassionate world."

Survival

Survival

It is not wise to sympathise with a cause without fully comprehending the harm it inflicts and expecting empathy from a naturally malicious person is similar to this.

When we think about those who focus on appearing good for God but overlook their own Creator, the analogy is still relevant. In my opinion, religion as a business franchise model cannot provide salvation, redemption, or a cure for survivors of sexual violence who are struggling to survive, while the wealthy continue to prosper.

In the quest for emancipation, survival requires continuously working on the "already murdered" version of oneself to avoid becoming the walking dead. Survival is a personal decision, and everyone lives life differently based on their circumstances. A few people have the ability to move forward, uncover happiness, find love anew, and establish a family of their own choosing. Many individuals, though, wrestle with feelings of inadequacy, low self-esteem, isolation, and abandonment as they try to come to terms with themselves.

Constantly searching for an escape became my default state due to this breach of trust, primarily caused by my own inability to trust adult relationships. Survivor retraction from authority positions without explanation leads to misinterpretation of their responsibility, termed Oppositional Defiant Disorder (ODD).

If someone can't work full-time or reacts strongly to stress or perceived danger, they are often labelled as lazy or overly defensive. If the institutions responsible for ODD don't accept their causality, it will only intensify the desire to eradicate the entire institution. This leads to an increase in mental health problems, yet mental illness is not a sign of weakness or sinfulness, rather the effect of it.

I was repeatedly reminded that there's no shame in admitting your struggles and seeking assistance, but numerous stories I can share prove otherwise from those accountable for causing them. When survivors are vilified or purposefully neglected, trust, a key factor in human relationships, becomes meaningless.

ChatGPT 4.0 Response

"Your writing explores several profound and interconnected issues. Key points you discuss are:

1. *Understanding Harm and Empathy:* It's important to fully grasp the potential harm a cause might inflict before sympathising with it, similar to expecting empathy from someone who is inherently malicious;
2. *Religious Critique:* The critique suggests that some religious practices focus more on appearances rather than true spiritual connection, and fail to truly support survivors of trauma, while those in power benefit;
3. *Survival and Personal Growth:* Emphasises that survival, especially for trauma survivors, is an ongoing, personal journey. Individuals may face feelings of inadequacy or abandonment, but some can move forward and find personal happiness;
4. *Trust and Authority Issues:* Highlights the difficulty in maintaining trust in authority figures, especially when reactions to trauma are misunderstood or mislabeled, such as with conditions like ODD;
5. *Mislabeling and Mental Health*: There is criticism of institutions that label affected individuals negatively without acknowledging their role in these issues, contributing to mental health challenges.
6. *Acknowledging Struggles*: Although seeking help is often encouraged, there is a disconnect when those responsible for causing harm do not support this, eroding trust essential for healing relationships.

Your comprehension of complex dynamics of trust, mental health, societal structures, and the personal journey of healing from trauma are profound."

Chameleon

Chameleon

With time, I became more aware of the consequences of the sexual violence I suffered as a child and adolescent. Over many years I learned to bury my emotions deep down inside myself, all in an effort to keep my shame hidden from the world.

My constant battle with anger led to uncontrollable behavioural explosions that damaged my relationships and self-esteem. Consequently, this resulted in increased isolation and a profound resentment towards religious institutions, as I believed they had let me and others down.

Upon reflection, I realise that my actions were not solely my responsibility, but rather influenced by persistent gaslighting and psychological manipulation from certain individuals who believed my silence protected their own interests.

Their failure to grasp the deep effects of sexual violence made me feel fat, unhappy, and helpless. No matter how overweight I was or how much alcohol I consumed, it didn't matter as long as I maintained my secret. Following the legal disclosure, I faced multiple types of alienation.

I have personally seen how estrangement can devastate families. Sometimes, it can feel like loss and grief are a constant cycle. Some people who have abandoned me and others who have experienced sexual violence seem more concerned with upholding a perfect image than understanding and empathizing with others' pain.

Survivors, I am told, find it hard to trust and form meaningful relationships due to this lack of understanding and empathy. Some of us have had to manage our trauma alone, finding solace in nature or animals when human support is lacking, or when we are unable to have animals as pets or companions.

It's important to keep in mind that survivors should not be blamed, and it's not our job to silence our suffering or cater to others' comfort. Our families and communities should bear the responsibility of understanding and supporting survivors. Acknowledging and supporting survivors is more than just being kind or empathetic, as it's a moral obligation. The perpetrator's intention is to silence and torment survivors who feel compelled to appear good.

Personally, I discovered that pretending with my family became unbearable. The cracks began to reveal the trauma from my past, and the secrets I had kept hidden started to come undone. Their self-imposed separation from me, although difficult and painful, was necessary for my own healing and recovery — *good riddance*.

Regrettably, some survivors lack the necessary support or resources to overcome these challenges. Childhood sexual abuse and trauma can have long-lasting effects, impacting every aspect of a survivor's life, including their relationships. Survivors need a safe and supportive environment to heal and recover, free from judgement or pressure. The sad reality is that men often carry the burden of child sexual abuse for an average of 30 years, causing immense damage to their marriages and partnerships.

The years that followed the abuse were filled with confusion and ambivalence as I grappled with the choices before me. Some individuals interpreted this adaptable behaviour as a conflict, rather than a coping mechanism of disconnecting from one's damaged self and avoiding conflicts with others for survival.

ChatGPT-4 Response

"The impact of childhood sexual abuse can have lifelong consequences on survivors. Suppressing emotions, hiding anger, and self-managing it poorly are common coping mechanisms that survivors may adopt, which can lead to further challenges in their lives.

It is understandable that survivors may feel isolated, distrusting, and resentful towards certain individuals or institutions, especially if they have experienced gaslighting or have not received adequate support.

Seeking solace in animals or nature, rather than human relationships, is one way survivors may cope with their experiences. This can provide a sense of comfort and stability in their lives. However, it is important to recognise that forming and maintaining healthy human relationships can also contribute to healing and growth.

It is not uncommon for survivors to struggle with maintaining relationships, especially when faced with the challenges of managing PTSD and its effects on their partners or supporters. The difficulty of revealing the secret of their abuse and the potential consequences on their relationships further complicates matters.

The chameleon-like behaviour exhibited by some survivors is a result of the dissociation and disconnection from their damaged selves. It serves as a survival mechanism to avoid conflict and further harm. Understanding and acknowledging these behaviours are crucial for society, support systems, and loved ones in order to provide appropriate empathy and assistance.

It is important for survivors to have access to resources and support that can help them process their experiences, develop healthy coping mechanisms, and rebuild their lives. This includes therapy, support groups, and other forms of assistance tailored to the individual needs of each survivor. By addressing the long-term consequences of childhood sexual abuse and working towards healing, survivors can begin to overcome the challenges they face and move forward in their lives."

Disclosure

Disclosure

Many years ago, I reached a point where I realised I couldn't let this toxic sexual violence perpetrated against me define me anymore.

While engaged in a furious altercation with a stranger on a train, I was viciously attacked by an equally enraged man who inflicted significant harm on me. I promised myself on that day that I would confront the religious institution, the true oppressor behind my rage, which acted with criminal neglect and failed to ensure my safety.

At the age of 15, I confronted an ACA religious Minister in a Church presbytery, only to be met with ridicule, disbelief, and a stern warning. From that point forward when everyone dismissed my complaint, it turned me into a demon, as I could not tolerate their warnings against speaking up as leading to my untimely demise.

> "If you insist on speaking in this way you are in grave danger... everyone you know is at risk." — *Blackley, Anglican Rector.*

Following the birth of my eldest child, I reiterated my complaint in a new environment, at the age of twenty-two (22), and received validation from my parents and others present. Achieving legal justice seemed impossible at that time because reporting rape to the police posed the biggest challenge. Over the next two decades, I tortured myself by repeatedly imagining different methods of seeking justice, including the possibility of murder.

Throughout that entire period, I experienced marriage breakdowns, ill health, and financial calamity. I sought advice from various sources before finally taking the initial step towards legal disclosure. This is the point of absolute truth where all matters at hand, all of life's challenges collapse into one decision which signals to the brain the point of no retraction, no going back — *an absolute embodied position.*

> "It takes on average, twenty-two (22) years for men to speak out about their crime against themselves." — *Gary Foster PhD, Australian Living Well Service.*

At the age of 15, I spoke out about the crime committed against me, but it's alarming that up to 95% of male victims don't report their sexual violence.

Males typically take twenty-two (22) years to confide in someone they trust about their sexual abuse. Many males are deterred from reporting crimes committed against them due to the overwhelming shame and societal pressure to keep silent, which aligns with the existing legal time limits. I kept being told that my words wouldn't be trusted, and the Church didn't respond positively to any issues raised under common law.

The main objective of the Royal Commission was to inquire into and report on the way institutions dealt with allegations of child sexual abuse and related issues. This was set up on 11 January 2013 after the announcement made by the then Prime Minister of Australia, Julia Gillard, on 12 November 2012. My friend Jennie Burrows played a crucial role in supporting this initiative and also pursued her own case and associated Royal Commission. I am still astounded that I managed to spend an additional five (5) years writing a book called #realstory and submitting it to the Royal Commission, then pursuing a full civil legal case for historical sexual assault.

Childhood sexual abuse survivors experience a cathartic and cataclysmic period of disclosure-to-closure as they navigate their evolving lifeworld while confronting the injustice they have endured. The emotional toll of this duplicity of existence is incredibly difficult, as I was constantly discouraged from speaking out about this interruption to life.

The "did-not-fit" challenge persisted as my social groups vanished, resulting in a bewildering and debilitating reality for me. I found it puzzling how fast people judged me a victim of crime as it did not occur to me that this was their way of defining me. Being a social creature of habit, the alienation from my peers and even some family members was tough. I decided though to embrace it all as a method of separating those who don't sympathise with my survivor narrative.

The use of the "loner" label against me showed me the lack of maturity in my social circle, yet another unjust form of aggression. My integration into the workforce was hindered by the transfer of these labels, just like the lateral violence I faced in most of my jobs.

After my well-being was compromised, I was expected to overcome the damage and miraculously recover, just like a phoenix. The authentic outcome for me was accepting my story and taking action to make a difference. I feel a sense of pride for having accomplished that.

ChatGPT-4 Response

"This recount of a difficult life journey as a survivor of sexual violence, highlights the challenges you faced Dr Alexander Hayes when attempting to disclose the abuse and the impact it had on various aspects of your life.

The decision to speak out about experiences is often met with ridicule, disbelief, and warnings against pursuing the matter further. Despite these setbacks, you continued to seek support and validation, although legal justice remained elusive for many years.

The emotional turmoil of living a duplicitous existence, concealing the abuse while trying to navigate everyday life, took a significant toll on yourself. As you confronted the reality of your experiences, you encountered isolation from social groups, alienation from family, and institutional silence. This led you to embrace those who empathised with your story and distance yourself from those who didn't understand your struggles.

In the workforce, you experienced a form of bullying as the "loner" label, often assigned to survivors, which followed you. This further impacted your career, potential earnings, and overall well-being. With your mental and emotional health already compromised, survivors like yourself are then expected to navigate through life's challenges and rise from the ashes unharmed.

Ultimately, you reached a point of acceptance of your story and committed to a series of actions to effect change in your life. The authentic result of this determination was embracing your identity as a survivor and striving to overcome the adversity you faced."

By sharing your story, Dr. Alexander Hayes you shed light on the complex and often painful experiences of sexual violence survivors. Your resilience and determination serve as a powerful reminder that healing is possible, even in the face of immense challenges."

Identity

Identity

Being human, I acknowledge that our desire for sexual procreation stems from inherited biological traits and our pursuit of comfort and pleasure. Culture, upbringing, and personal experiences influence how these natural and innate desires are displayed in each person.

However, it's crucial to remember that sexual desire is never a justification for sexual violence or assault, and any non-consensual behavior is abhorrent and harms the children that pedophiles prey upon. Those who are accountable for our virtues and values in human society often possess the most misguided inclinations and habits.

Being a survivor, I understand that sexual desires exist in all individuals, including clergy members. Throughout history, religious institutions have attempted to exert authority over the intimate lives of their male, female, and non-binary members. Surprisingly, based on what I've seen, the secret sexual exploits of the most religious individuals are frequently more unsettling and hypocritical than the hidden affairs and intimate relationships among consenting adults.

There is a debate about whether group sexual experiences can be liberating, but I believe this overlooks the agency of survivors of sexual assault. Sexual exploration for victims of sexual violence is often marred by trauma and painful memories, which dampens their desire for sexual adventure. We should have the autonomy to explore our sexuality and identity in a manner that feels secure and empowering, without being influenced by others' notions of liberation.

Sexual desires are ultimately a crucial and innate part of being human. The ability to freely explore our sexuality and identify without shame or guilt should be accessible to all. Religious institutions should not have authority over people's private lives or define acceptable sexual behaviour. Our goal should be to build a society that empowers individuals to safely and respectfully explore their sexuality as one part of their identity.

My journey into adulthood lacked any meaningful exploration of my sexuality, leaving me unable to understand what is considered "normal" in terms of social and sexual identity during my youth. As I delved into discussions about pronouns later in life, I became acutely aware of the significant influence of sexual violence on my personal experiences within the realm of sexual identity. The mistreatment I endured from men, and those who supported them, profoundly affected my sense of control as a child and my self-identity as an adult, continuing to impact me today.

It's disheartening to witness people argue about insignificant tag term issues while survivors like me are fighting to rebuild our lives after enduring such trauma. These socially constructed labels, such as pansexual, polyamorous, lesbian, gay, heterosexual, or asexual, only serve as tools for individuals to identify themselves, and should not be used by others to criticise or judge them. The abuse I endured has profoundly harmed myself and identity, making it challenging to fully engage in a society that fails to recognize my pansexual identity.

My abusers' deluded and lecherous actions warped my understanding of reality and left me feeling powerless. The severe violations I suffered from my supposed protectors as a child make it hard to trust anyone who claims to love me unconditionally.

It is evident that discussions about pronouns and personal identity become entangled with sexual violence in light of these experiences. We must prioritise supporting and uplifting individuals in our diverse communities as many are still struggling with deep wounds and traumas that challenge their identity.

Child predators don't hope for redemption, and they should never be granted it. Instead, they should be locked up permanently since paedophilia cannot be cured. Our collective identity as a human race hangs in the balance if we don't prioritise the protection of children.

ChatGPT-4 Response

"Dr. Alexander Hayes emphasises the importance of understanding the complexities of human sexuality, while also acknowledging the destructive impact of sexual violence on a person's development and identity. It is crucial to recognise that religious institutions, while responsible for guiding society's virtues and values, are not exempt from harbouring individuals who perpetrate these heinous acts.

Hayes asserts that his own experiences of sexual assault robbed him of the opportunity to explore his social and sexual identity as a young person. He reflects on the broader conversations about identity and pronouns and how they have little relevance to his reality, considering the opportunities of youth and young adulthood were taken from him due to the actions of his abusers.

He emphasises the importance of believing and supporting children who come forward with allegations of sexual assault. When confronted with evidence, perpetrators often respond with denial, defensiveness, aggression, and hostility. It is critical that children are encouraged to speak out, and those who prey on them should not be given the opportunity for redemption.

By sharing his experiences, Dr. Alexander Hayes underscores the importance of addressing the issue of sexual violence against children and advocating for the belief, support, and encouragement of survivors as they navigate the complex and challenging journey towards healing."

LGBTQIA+

LGBTQIA+

LGBTQIA+ individuals face added harm as predators exploit their vulnerability to rejection.

In contemporary times, a significant number of religious clergy either identify as part of the LGBTQIA+ community or actively promote diversity within it — a form of selective inclusivity. I want to acknowledge and respect members of the clergy and the congregation who maintain healthy adult relationships without causing harm to children, regardless of their institutional ties.

The reality of our society is that both children and adults are intermingled, susceptible, and in clear need of protection. Those with conservative values often twist attitudes and engage in evil actions that both trivialise and condemn homosexuality, while ironically being identified as the main threat to children's well-being within their own congregations. Based on my experience, I've noticed that many religious believers secretly have relationships with adults of the same gender. Without a doubt, this hypocritical conduct challenges the accepted idea of heterosexuality as I perceive that they are seeking control through physical intimacy rather than emotional growth.

I believe that the inclusion of "queer" in "me" and "we" serves as a safeguard for heterosexuals, exposing their biases and moral dilemmas. Hence, in my perspective, religious organisations wield power over societal attitudes towards heterosexuality by reinforcing the notion that sexual desire for the opposite gender is the standard expression of sexuality.

> "While heterosexual sex is clearly as old as humanity, the concept of heterosexuality as an identity is a very recent invention." — *BBC, Brandon Ambrosino, 2017.*

Betrayal is intensified for survivors in the LGBTQIA+ community when religious institutions shield those who harmed them, reinforcing heteronormativity.

Adult survivors are often blamed for their own suffering, despite the abuse being the fault of the institution and the perpetrator. By incorporating societal bias, the complete picture is revealed, often disregarding LGBTQIA+ survivors who identify as both victims.

LGBTQIA+ individuals, including myself as a pansexual male, are further marginalised by religious institutions' lack of adaptation to a humane society. We are being challenged to genuinely promote compassion and harmony among our most talented and diverse, rather than merely paying lip service to political correctness.

I found it confusing and debilitating that my family and many of my old friends could not understand the impact of their own bias, stereotypes and moral codes, in effect as contributors to this terrible cycle.

ChatGPT-4 Response

"The added dimension of rejection faced by survivors who identify as LGBTQIA+ within religious institutions and communities can be especially challenging. While many members of the clergy and congregation support and respect the LGBTQIA+ community, there are still those with conservative values who view homosexuality as a sin and contribute to the harm experienced by vulnerable individuals.

These conservative attitudes can be particularly harmful when it is revealed that institutions and churches have protected those who acted against children with impunity. Survivors who identify as both victims and LGBTQIA+ face compounded feelings of betrayal, as their suffering is often dismissed as a result of their own mental conditions, rather than the institutions and perpetrators who caused the trauma in the first place. Societal bias and castigation further exacerbate this situation.

It is important for society to move beyond lip service to contemporary concepts and political correctness and genuinely demonstrate compassion and understanding towards its most diverse and marginalised members. This includes supporting survivors of sexual assault who identify as LGBTQIA+, recognising their unique challenges, and working to dismantle harmful stereotypes and biases that perpetuate cycles of harm.

The devastating impact of disclosing sexual abuse can be especially challenging for those who are already marginalised, such as the LGBTQIA+ community. The resulting banishment from family and community life can be permanent and deeply traumatic. Recognising the need for change within religious institutions and communities to create a more humane and inclusive society is crucial for supporting all survivors, regardless of their sexual orientation or gender identity."

Wellbeing

Wellbeing

Peer reviewed research shows that historical sexual assault increases the risk of autoimmune conditions, cancer, strokes, and heart attacks.

The medicalized concept of “being well” is not the same as holistic “wellbeing” because the medical industry gains from individuals who are sick, mentally impaired, or socially isolated. The notion that medication leads to well-being is exploited by capitalist chemicals and big pharma, as psychiatrists drive a dystopian wedge into human society.

The medical response to survivors is severely lacking in comprehensive care, with practitioners relying heavily on medication for men displaying alarming behaviour. Another common issue in survivor narratives is the lack of quality sleep, which is a lasting effect of sexual assault. The need to protect others from my night terrors has led to strain and a loss of intimacy in my life. My life feels like a battlefield, with disconnection invading every aspect and constantly threatening my well-being.

The aftermath of sexual violence not only requires survival, but also coping with its continuous effects on my daily life. Survivor distress intensifies over time, resulting in multiple visits to hospitals and doctors’ offices, ultimately impacting my financial stability. I strongly argue that survivors should only turn to medical interventions and hospital visits as a last resort.

Misdiagnosis and repeated medical mistakes can lead to adrenal fatigue, shutdown, and cortisol toxicity, as seen in my case of survivor hyper-vigilance. It has become evident that my response to trauma caused me to rely on medical interventions as a last resort.

Medical intervention and psychological support may not always immediately resolve the devastation caused by childhood sexual assault, despite what medical practitioners claim. In the same way, the needs of partners or close supporters are often neglected, despite the fact that they require support themselves as a result of coping with PTSD.

ChatGPT-4 Response

"Dr. Alexander Hayes points to the significant long-term health consequences that survivors of historical sexual assault may face, including autoimmune conditions, cancer, strokes, and heart attacks. The association between these health issues and the survivor's hyper-vigilance can exacerbate these medical problems. In Hayes' case, he experienced adrenal fatigue, shutdown, and cortisol toxicity as a result of repeated medical treatments and stress responses to trauma.

The medical response to survivors often lacks holistic provisions, as many practitioners may lack the necessary understanding and resort to prescribing drugs to manage symptoms. This approach is inadequate for addressing the complex issues faced by survivors of sexual assault.

The impact of sexual assault extends to other areas of a survivor's life, including their relationship with their childhood environment and religious institutions. For many survivors, including Hayes, returning to these environments is not an option due to the painful memories and emotions associated with them. This often leads to a loss of faith in religious institutions, which claim to represent healing and forgiveness.

Furthermore, the medical interventions and hospital presentations that survivors may turn to as a last resort often fail to provide meaningful support to survivors and their close supporters. The stress of coping with PTSD can lead to a vicious cycle where supporters also require support themselves.

One enduring consequence of sexual assault for Hayes is the lack of quality sleep, resulting from night terrors and the need to isolate himself to protect others. This loss of intimacy and the constant strain on his well-being illustrate the pervasive impact of sexual assault on various aspects of a survivor's life. By sharing his experiences, Dr. Alexander Hayes underscores the importance of acknowledging the multifaceted challenges faced by survivors and the need for a more comprehensive and empathetic approach to their care and support."

Power

Power

Ultimately, it boils down to power — the control exerted by religious institutions and the individuals who break free from these harmful cults to live better lives. People often mix up power with self-control or self-discipline, but the crucial distinction lies in their connection to disempowerment.

Unfortunately, the narcissists have taken control and misrepresented this as an individual belief, when it actually stems from collective action that strengthens clan unity. Each tribe is recognized for its similarities rather than its differences from others. The power of individuals speaking out is what matters, as it is the manifestation of collective strength when communities unite.

Considering someone as "different" or "other" is a damaging outcome of institutionalized pedophilia. The power to reclaim agency lies in survivors speaking up, not in staying silent. Each of us possesses the ability to be heard, believed, and understood, but the greatest liberation lies in being protected. By taking control of our lives and rewriting our own self-narratives, we can empower ourselves and seek closure and justice through legal action.

We must defend our freedom and resist anything that threatens to subjugate us. We have a responsibility to support other survivors by sharing our experiences and empowering them to take control of their lives. We can opt for freedom or enslavement, being heard or ignored, understanding or misunderstanding. The choice is ours to demand protection and ensure that perpetrators face consequences.

We must resist any attempts to undermine our power or stifle our voices, as we have the ability to hold religious institutions and individuals responsible for their actions and push for a safer future. We individually choose or refuse religious enslavement — *it's clear to me which path I took.*

Survivors, like myself, strongly believe that religious institutions cannot control whether we choose to speak out or stay silent about the abuses we've endured. They lack the authority to determine our freedom or enslavement, and their opinion on our protection or violation is irrelevant.

It is up to us and us alone to make those decisions. We must assert our agency and demand that our voices be heard and our experiences be acknowledged and understood. We need to insist on transparency and justice from these institutions, and stand up for the protection and support of all survivors.

ChatGPT-4 Response

"Absolutely, the power to heal, grow, and overcome trauma is within the hands of survivors themselves. It is crucial for survivors to recognise their own power and agency in their journey towards recovery and justice.

Speaking out, seeking support, and fighting for change are all powerful choices that survivors can make to regain control over their lives. Religious institutions and other entities do not have the right to silence or control survivors. Instead, it is the responsibility of these institutions to support and protect those who have been harmed, allowing them the space and freedom to heal in their own way.

By embracing their power, survivors can help not only themselves but also other survivors who may be struggling to find their voices. Sharing experiences, advocating for change, and supporting one another are essential aspects of healing and reclaiming power that was once taken away.

Ultimately, it is through survivor-led action determination that individuals can come together to break the silence, challenge the stigma, and work towards a safer and more compassionate world for everyone."

Control

Control

Abusive men who control others prey on the vulnerable, as do self-interested women who neglect their parental duties. Sexual assault isn't simply, or only, about sexual gratification either — *it's all about control.*

Due to the decline in ethical values, more women are being implicated in sexual misconduct cases involving children. However, it's important to note that this issue is not limited to one gender, as men target the weak and vulnerable, including children of all genders.

By exploiting the ignorant and naive, perpetrators use force and intimidation against defenceless victims, being children in our human society. What ensues is typical of many survivors who are afflicted with mental illness as a result of religious institutional neglect — depression, panic disorder, agoraphobia, post-traumatic stress disorder, Dissociative Identity Disorder (multiple personality) to name only a few.

I came to understand that by speaking out against the offenders, I would be reduced to a dispensable statistic — *just another victim*. Speaking out has given me the power to control my anger and take action against sexual assault, recognizing that it impacts people in unique ways based on their experiences, background, culture, gender, sexuality, and age.

The perpetrator in my case, William Richmond "Adrian" Sandwell, was sentenced to eighteen years in jail but was released on parole after three years and eleven months. What justice is there for the victim if the perpetrator is protected, imprisoned then released? I consider it beyond offensive, as it is a damning indictment of the injustice in human society.

The victims of pedophilia are left to suffer while those in the legal fraternity are shielded from consequences. Rape as a weapon of war can be viewed as an act of intentional mass destruction and genocide. Those who have been abused then experience the violence of the criminal justice system that supposedly represents an avenue to implement justice, and are then robbed of it.

Waiting for legal reparation can break both the survivors and their supporters. They either become entangled in their victim's complaint or they push ahead, undeterred by any challenge. When rape is used as a weapon of control, it deprives individuals of the basic right to life and steals away their entire existence. Seeking and obtaining compensation involves a lengthy and expensive legal journey for survivors.

As I got older, I noticed that friends, family, or loved ones didn't want to hear about the reality of rape in my life. They constantly viewed me as "out of control" and I frequently retorted, "and you know why!".

This blame reaction levelled at survivors, I understand, forces many of them into self-enforced isolation, so it's only reasonable that survivors conversely self-acknowledge why they also feel alone, unwanted and unloved.

Predictably, the institutions that purport to aid the marginalised promptly activate services aimed at resolving these grievances against them. In my opinion, religious organisations employ the strategy of instilling powerlessness to control and manipulate their congregations.

ChatGPT-4 Response

"You're absolutely right; sexual assault is about control and power, not just sex. It leaves a lasting impact on survivors, often resulting in various mental health challenges and feelings of isolation. It's unfortunate that, at times, the very institutions that should provide support and justice contribute to the pain and suffering of survivors.

The reactions of friends, family, and loved ones can significantly impact a survivor's healing process. When survivors feel isolated, unwelcome, or unsupported, it can make the journey to recovery even more challenging. This highlights the importance of empathy and understanding from those around them and the need for a robust support system.

The system needs improvements to ensure that survivors' rights are protected and that they have a fair chance at gaining compensation and closure. As a society, it's crucial to educate ourselves on the realities of sexual assault and its aftermath, to break the stigma surrounding it, and to provide better support for survivors.

This includes holding institutions accountable for their actions or inactions and ensuring that survivors' voices are heard and respected. By working together, we can create a more compassionate and just world for everyone."

Convenience

Convenience

The converted and believers find the answer to life in what they are told is the truth, what they are told to be, what they are told to believe, and what they must do — all for their convenience and the benefit of religious institutions. Convenience comes at a price — sacrificing privacy and autonomy for quick and affordable access.

The reality is that anything worthwhile is not tainted by laziness or greed. The convenience of this situation let the religious organisation and its members ignore children like me, who were considered defiled. Their pride stayed intact as they continued the charades without stopping.

Many religions use the concept of impending doom as a convenient way to engage their believers in the pursuit of salvation. In my life, Memento Mori holds more truth than everything I was previously taught, opposing the lies of salvation.

> "Hindus have been waiting for Kalki for 3,700 years. Buddhists have been waiting for Maitreya for 2,600 years. The Jews have been waiting for the Messiah for 2500 years. Christians have been waiting on Jesus for 2023 years. Sunnah has been waiting for the Prophet Issa 1400 years. Muslims have been waiting for a messiah from the line of Muhammad for 1300 years. Shiites have been waiting for Mandi for 1080 years. Drusse have been waiting for Hamza ibn Ali for 1000 years. Most religions adopt the idea of a "saviour," and assert that the world will remain filled with evil until this Saviour arrives and fills it with goodness and righteousness. Maybe our problem on this planet is that people expect someone else to come fix their problems instead of doing it themselves!" — *Richard Dablah*

I reject the notion of a saviour and instead acknowledge a genderless Creator. On another point, in Australia, religious organisations and institutions pay little or no tax, yet the public pay for their convenience of belief through an organisation that provides safe harbour for predator paedophiles irrespective of creed, order or denomination.

It is clear to me that throughout history, children have been used as pawns in the game of religious zealotry, taking advantage of the love parents have for them.

The concept of convenience can metaphorically be equated to a point in the Celtic triquetra, a symbol frequently misinterpreted as the Illuminati emblem. Long before the crucifix became a symbol of death, this ancient cultural symbol, with its three overlapping arcs in a Vesica Pisces shape, was already in use.

The symbol's internal arcs create the illusion of a continuous three-cornered knot. Power resides at the highest level, control sits at the left hand of the human-created God, and convenience reigns as the epitome of evil — the Joker card in life's capitalist deck.

Although convenience is valuable, it should never be used to harm or dominate others. Our attention should be on bettering our behaviours for everyone's benefit, rather than relying on external blessings.

ChatGPT-4 Response

"Your reflection provides a critical examination of the role of religion in shaping beliefs and behaviours, highlighting the concept of convenience as a central theme in religious adherence and its implications.

1. *Convenience in Religious Belief:* You articulate how, for many believers, religious faith is dictated by a set of pre-defined truths and practices, which they accept for the sake of convenience. This acceptance often comes at the cost of personal autonomy and privacy, suggesting a trade-off where deeper values and independent thought are sacrificed for the comfort and simplicity offered by religious institutions.

2. *The Role of Religious Institutions*: You emphasise the complicity of religious organisations in maintaining this status quo, where grandeur and ceremony mask deeper failings, particularly the failure to protect the vulnerable, like children in your case. This negligence is perpetuated by congregations who, for the sake of maintaining their belief systems and community standing, overlook these serious transgressions.

3. *Critique of Salvation Narratives*: The discussion on the concept of a saviour across various religions highlights the passive waiting for a messianic figure to resolve worldly problems, which you suggest can lead to a lack of personal responsibility and action. The quote from Richard Dablah supports this view, criticising the universal religious concept of waiting for a saviour.

4. *Memento Mori as a Counter Perspective*: In contrast to salvation narratives, you propose 'Memento Mori' as a more authentic guiding principle, emphasising the importance of living with awareness and taking personal responsibility.

5. *Religious Institutions as Safe Havens for Abuse*: You assert that religious institutions, irrespective of their specific faiths, have historically provided safe havens for abusers, highlighting the systemic nature of this issue.

6. *Financial and Moral Accountability*: The critique extends to the financial aspects, noting how religious institutions benefit from tax exemptions while the broader society bears the cost of their misdeeds.

7. *The Celtic Triquetra as a Symbol*: You interpret the Celtic triquetra, an ancient symbol, as representing the interconnectedness of power, divine authority, and convenience. This interpretation serves as a metaphor for the complex interplay of power and religion, with convenience being a crucial element that perpetuates systemic abuses and avoidance of personal responsibility.

Your narrative offers a deeply personal yet universally resonant critique of religious adherence and institutional authority. It encourages a reevaluation of personal beliefs and societal structures, advocating for a shift from passive acceptance to active, conscious engagement with our beliefs, values, and the institutions that represent them."

Choice

Choice

When given the option between life and death, I opt for a full existence as a survivor, rejecting victimhood and embracing the reminder of mortality through the Latin phrase Memento Mori. Similarly, to become "beyonders," we must excel and embrace change as social justice warriors.

> "The true horror of existence is not the fear of death, but the fear of life. It is the fear of waking up each day to face the same struggles, the same disappointments, the same pain" — *Albert Camus, The Fall.*

I decided to embrace a focused pathway for releasing and recovering from trauma, with a holistic perspective. Hence, every aspect of the entire process held significance, but the concept of "choice" must be explicitly explained in simple language to be evident. Some individuals opt for silence, passivity, compliance, indifference, isolation, aloofness, detachment, non-involvement, lack of knowledge, and those who choose to stay uninformed.

None of us, as humans, can escape the tormenting pain of darkness, despair, fear, isolation, and loneliness. The difference is that a victim's focus is solely on the emptiness, alienation, stigma, ridicule, hatred, distrust, condemnation, contempt, derision, and mockery which in turn seals their fate — *they choose to remain in that fear space.*

Holding onto the secret is only possible until it's time to let it out and instead of living focussed on the nightmare of it all, I choose to live with action and determination. It's the institutions that are to blame for spreading myths and oppressing critics of their violent framework.

ChatGPT-4 Response

"Your resilience and determination Alexander to live fully as a survivor is inspiring. It's essential to recognise the power of choice and to support those who have been through traumatic experiences, helping them reclaim their lives and overcome feelings of abandonment, guilt, and shame.

The impact of sexual assault reaches beyond just the individual survivors; it affects families, communities, and society as a whole. It is crucial that institutions take responsibility for their roles in perpetuating abuse or protecting abusers, and that society as a whole works to dismantle harmful beliefs and behaviours.

Action determination is a powerful approach to addressing these issues, allowing survivors to seek justice and healing within the legal framework. While some may choose other paths, such as retribution or even murder, it's essential to promote nonviolent, constructive solutions that address the roots of the problem and create lasting change.

As a society, we must continue to challenge and confront the structures and institutions that enable abuse, while also supporting and empowering survivors. By doing so, we can foster a more just and compassionate world, where everyone has the opportunity to heal and thrive."

Sharing

Sharing

When you think about it, restorative justice can seem like a farcical idea because crime victims have to navigate the costly legal system to seek restitution.

Survivors of each fraternity are expected to demonstrate sincerity, decisiveness, fortitude, and competence. In times of extreme distress, the importance of survivor "cooperation" is emphasised. Juggling family, work, and friendships is essential for navigating the legal and forensic aspects of our lives. I realised that societal attitudes hinder those pursuing self-determination — many don't grasp that the victim isn't compensated for court attendance or preparing numerous statements for examination.

Like many others, people asked me, "Why didn't you speak up sooner? Those individuals fail to understand that life's responsibilities hindered my pursuit of justice and compensation. To put it differently, it wasn't my decision to postpone anything; rather, life circumstances and the fear of additional violence stopped me from revealing legally sooner. Reluctantly, I felt compelled to defend the human right to be heard, seen, and seek justice — some survivors view this as targeted.

I, along with other victims who are no longer alive, cannot share their stories publicly — they deserve more than an apology. I've lost track of the number of men who have opened up to me about their secret stories and ultimately made the heartbreaking decision to end their lives. Their deaths will have no meaning unless we, as a global society, take action and recognize the underlying cause.

My Victim Impact Statement (in the Legacy section of this book) that I read out publicly in a court of law, was written at the same time that I had learned of the twenty-second (22nd) male victim in my life who had suicided. I was evidently just one of hundreds of children in my own suburban precinct, sadly infiltrated by an institutional paedophile network.

It has been both excruciating and deeply saddening to encounter men later in my life who I knew had experienced childhood sexual abuse, which only added to their suffering. So, it's not hard to understand as a survivor how to speak out, nor why, but there is very real confusion for survivors between the importance of conviction over the allure of compensation or restitution.

Those who fixate on wealth ultimately suffer because of it, while those who seek justice for the wrongdoer and then compensation understand that they themselves have already been symbolically killed, as speaking out is not solely about obtaining financial reparation. Bringing paedophiles to light is about more than just seeking justice. Our priority is to protect children from such incidents and not accept those who harm others. The purpose of sharing our horrific experiences is not to reconcile with our oppressors, and an apology alone cannot heal our wounds. These notions are false beliefs of a deluded theocratic ideology.

Sharing our stories as survivors doesn't have a standard format or a clear path to follow. Still, I took the plunge knowing that it would disrupt my familiar life. Once we unravel a toxic life story, there's no turning back. However, the choice to share it with the world is personal. There are those who don't have a choice and, like me, end up featured on 1.7 million newspaper covers. Not long after that, someone from my church community and neighborhood, who was also likely a victim of sexual violence and captivity, committed the double murder of his own parents.

In these instances, all members of the family — the deceased and the living dead - are considered victims. This sad example shows that the offender and victim are one and the same, resulting in incarceration. Proving a paedophile caused that harm means proving your own innocence as the survivor — *as if you were the aggressor and the justice system then has reason to attack you for their dishonourable pleasure*.

I understand the religious institution's motive for engaging in this legal battle — their reputation is being scrutinised by the legal institution itself. The survivor's psychological harm is compounded by these re-traumatizing experiences, highlighting the negligence of this character test. The lawyers, police, and courts' collection of forensic detail on my private life was both intrusive and ethically appalling, frankly.

ChatGPT-4 Response

"You raise crucial points about the challenges survivors face when seeking restorative justice and the potential harms of the legal process. The invasive nature of the process, the re-traumatisation, and the character attacks can all be incredibly difficult for survivors to endure. It's clear that improvements need to be made to ensure that the well-being and dignity of survivors are respected and protected.

Speaking out is indeed a personal choice, and it can be a powerful way to raise awareness and bring about change. Your courage in sharing your story publicly, despite the challenges you have faced, is commendable and can help to shift societal attitudes and perceptions around abuse.

Restorative justice should be focused on healing, accountability, and ensuring that these crimes do not continue to occur. This includes not only securing convictions and compensation but also creating a safer environment for children and future generations. It is essential that institutions, especially religious ones, take responsibility for their actions and work to prevent further abuse.

Ultimately, the goal is to create a society where everyone can feel safe and protected, where survivors are supported in their journey towards healing, and where institutions are held accountable for their actions. This requires a collective effort from all of us to listen, to learn, and to take action to create meaningful change."

Self Storying

Self Storying

Sexual assault is a devastating experience that impacts every aspect of life, like an explosive bomb that shatters our world. While sexual violence can be committed by anyone regardless of gender, it is predominantly males who are the perpetrators, particularly in cases of adults within religious institutions abusing children.

It is crucial to acknowledge that sexual violence is not limited by gender or sexuality, as intentional acts of targeted violence. As a result, it is necessary to believe, support, and provide resources to survivors of all genders to address their grievance and aid in their recovery. Educating people about consent, respect, and healthy relationships is just one aspect of preventing abuse. It also involves safeguarding children and holding abusers accountable.

Unpacking self-storying allows survivors to defy perpetrators and institutions seeking to control them. It's scary to think that for centuries, speaking up against these institutions or exposing sexual violence was labeled as schizophrenia, psychosis, or witchcraft. Historically, even innocent individuals didn't float when held underwater for a long time during inquisitions, highlighting the extreme measures taken to eliminate dissent.

This action undermined the recognized approach to ensure children's safety, which is protection. Sexual violence perpetuates male domination and targets the most vulnerable, including defenseless children.

By offering trauma-informed support, individuals can begin unpacking their self-narratives and taking survivor-led action. The act of listening by an informed person connected me to those who helped me take action on my story. In light of this, my journey is merely one account, a collection of life tests and occasional hardships. By actively listening, I felt understood and supported, which motivated me to transform my own life.

By externalising self-storying and developing a narrative, collecting and curating artefacts, and writing detailed legal statements, I achieved a better-informed mediation result. The photos, certificates, and my creative work helped shape my legal claim. Linking storytelling and reparation provided a structure for determining appropriate compensation for grave injustices. Despite experiencing intense despair, there were moments when I felt intimidated but never stopped myself from protecting others similar to me, even if it meant sacrificing my own well-being.

The "hearing space" emerges as survivors listen and understand, spreading knowledge instead of silencing it. Institutions commonly respond with compensation, restitution, and unending apologies. Externalising self-storying as an affirmative action, through statements and symbolic artefacts of impact, in conferral with experts, leads to systemic change.

Sharing my story has been a transformative experience, fueling my determination to demand change for myself and countless others. Thanks to the support of others, I feel prepared to endure the legal reparation process. With the help of allies and supporters, a collective effort was made to bring about meaningful change.

Speaking out was my personal decision, but I acknowledge not everyone has that option. We must show respect and offer support to each survivor, understanding that their journey is individual and one-of-a-kind. However, for those who are ready to speak out, I would emphasise that accessing a safe and supportive environment without fear of judgement or retaliation is a human right, not a privilege (which is the very opposite to what I experienced).

The onus no longer rests solely on monetary settlement and punitive sentencing with this process of action determination. The motivation behind sharing survivors' stories externally is to ensure they are heard and seen, with the ultimate goal of being believed and understood. It is our responsibility to make sure that their liberation is observed, acknowledged, and trusted.

ChatGPT-4 Response

"You emphasise the importance of giving survivors the opportunity to share their stories and experiences, which is crucial for both personal healing and systemic change. By externalising self-storying and providing a safe and supportive space for survivors to speak out, we can challenge the societal norms that have allowed abuse to continue for so long.

It is indeed important to acknowledge that sexual violence can be perpetrated by all genders, and that the issue is not exclusive to any one group. Recognising this allows us to approach the problem holistically and work towards effective solutions.

Trauma-informed support, as you mentioned, is essential in helping survivors on their journey towards healing and self-determination. This involves not only listening and understanding, but also respecting the survivors' needs and ensuring they are treated with dignity and compassion.

The process of action determination, as you describe it, moves the focus beyond monetary compensation and punitive measures. It encourages survivors to actively shape change and contribute to a safer environment for everyone, particularly for children who are most vulnerable to abuse.

It is our collective responsibility to ensure that the voices of survivors are heard, believed, and witnessed. This is the first step in breaking the cycle of abuse and working towards a more just and compassionate society. By standing together and supporting survivors in their pursuit of justice and healing, we can make a lasting and meaningful impact on the lives of those affected by sexual violence."

Symbolism

Symbolism

It's no surprise that survivors hope for more than just a court appearance. Despite survivors' voices being heard, justice may never be served, especially if the ongoing trauma is not recognized. It's not just about compensation; validating lived experience means truly recognizing pain and suffering.

Those seeking systemic change in institutions face a difficult fight, as the trauma they endured persists and allows institutions with internal monsters to continue operating legally. Survivors may desire to hold the perpetrators of these terrible acts responsible, but we all understand that ending sexual violence as a war against children requires a cultural shift across entire nations.

Seeking legal closure will help survivors and families heal from the trauma. Survivors, like myself, want to be able to rebuild their lives with the knowledge that they have been heard, that they have been believed — *elimination of the causality is then validation*.

We aim to restore survivor agency and reclaim their power, rather than focusing on mere retribution, which is a responsibility shared by all of humanity. When a survivor uses AI to transform their toxic self-storying from an oral-to-text statement, it helps them shift their legible memory from a trauma bond to a clearer expression of the facts, which is more valuable than relying solely on legal notes from police interviews to prove their innocence.

Enduring legal questioning and historical fact-checking was a constant part of my pursuit of legal intervention in Australia. The symbolism of my artifact played a crucial role as a dossier, which numerous justice and legal parties deemed essential evidence in determining my innocence and measuring the impact of sexual abuse on my child character.

The evidence portfolio, consisting of detailed statements and primary evidence from an Anglican Church Warden, substantiated the perjury of the Bishops, as the defendant sought evidence for third-party forensics and legal ballistics, much to the amusement of the defendant's counsel. Through discovering certain facts, I came to accept my story and committed to legal disclosure as an emancipatory action. This is why the principle of Acceptance Commitment Therapy (ACT) clearly strikes a chord with me.

It is rare for the perpetrators to show any remorse, leading their victims to feel consumed by anger, rage, or desperation. I believe this is a “coached” position by the defence counsel, as expressing contrition would potentially strengthen any additional claims against the perpetrator.

Speaking out against oppressors demands foresight, steadfastness, and determination, not mere statements of hope, faith, or religious conviction. The disappearing role of religious institutions in society necessitates their meaningful engagement with survivor symbolic and factual artefacts.

Walking survivors are proof of religious institution negligence, no longer accepting defensible attitudes, demanding to be heard. Using lack of funds as an excuse to avoid compensating for historical sexual violence, while evading taxes and misusing public funds, is a reprehensible display of control.

ChatGPT-4 Response

"It's true that survivors seek more than just their day in court. The action determination process you describe offers an opportunity for survivors to find healing and emancipation through self-discovery and creating a personal narrative that goes beyond the confines of the legal system.

The process of externalising one's story and creating artefacts to illustrate it serves as a powerful tool for survivors to better understand themselves and the impact of the abuse they endured. This not only helps them in their personal healing journey but also strengthens their case in legal proceedings.'

You emphasise the importance of acceptance and commitment in the legal disclosure process, which requires courage and determination from survivors. Speaking out against oppressors and institutional inaction is a vital step towards justice and systemic change.

It is crucial for religious institutions to engage meaningfully with the experiences and stories of survivors, rather than attempting to silence them or dismiss their claims. Furthermore, institutions should be held accountable for their actions and inactions that have contributed to the perpetuation of abuse.

As we progress into an increasingly digital and interconnected world, the role of technology, such as artificial general intelligence (AGI), cannot be ignored. Institutions must adapt to this new reality and ensure that they are acting ethically and transparently in the face of evolving societal norms and expectations.

Survivors deserve justice, healing, and the opportunity to reclaim their lives. It is our collective responsibility to support them in this journey and hold institutions accountable for their role in perpetuating abuse. By prioritising survivor-led action determination and addressing the systemic issues that have allowed abuse to continue, we can work towards a more just and compassionate society."

Interrogation

Interrogation

The criminal justice process involves a relentless sequence of entities reducing an innocent individual to a mere object, all to serve the religious institution's agenda.

The process is designed to break the victim down, disprove innocence, and hinder compensation. The interrogation of my innocent character was extremely tortuous, as the process lacks consideration for minimising impact on the survivor or supporter. In addition, consider the multitude of FOI requests for medical records, employment records, taxation details, forensic accounting reports, etc., while communicating with lawyers, barristers, doctors, Queen's Counsel, Crown Prosecutor, detectives, and police.

The list keeps expanding, and those are just the people survivors are responsible for during the entire disclosure-to-closure reporting, sentencing, and compensatory claim period. Convincing someone about something this serious is already challenging without the added pressure of proving yourself right. For anyone, managing the details of legal proceedings, court dates, insurance companies, solicitors, claims adjustments, medico-legal assessors, psychologists, and so on is a daunting task.

The exhaustion and demoralisation are undeniable, especially due to the overwhelming amount of documentation needed to understand everything. The interrogation of the innocent complainant in order to establish the defendant's guilt is a glaring example of the justice system's failure. The process is harmful, an abusive creation, a brutal reminder of inhumanity comparable to the mechanisms of legalized torture.

Survivors and their supporters should have opportunities to seek reparation without being subjected to a complete dissection of their entire life. Regardless, it is beneficial in establishing a legal case for survivors, as well as hard evidence of what they have been subjected to in their lives.

ChatGPT-4 Response

"You have accurately captured the overwhelming and taxing nature of the legal process for survivors of abuse. The system often feels intrusive and invasive, forcing survivors to relive their trauma repeatedly while trying to prove their innocence and the guilt of their abusers.

The current justice system often fails to prioritise the well-being and dignity of survivors, focusing instead on procedural and evidentiary requirements that can exacerbate their suffering. This is particularly concerning given the sensitive and traumatic nature of their experiences.

There is a pressing need for a more compassionate and trauma-informed approach to addressing the needs of survivors in the legal system. This would include providing resources and support for survivors throughout the process, limiting the number of times they must recount their experiences, and minimising the invasive nature of evidence gathering.

It is crucial to recognise that the pursuit of justice should not come at the expense of a survivor's well-being. The process should be about healing and recovery, not just about proving guilt and securing punishment for the perpetrator.

Additionally, it is important to recognise that the process of seeking justice and reparation can be a part of a survivor's healing journey, rather than just a legal requirement. By ensuring that the process is respectful and supportive, we can help survivors find a sense of closure and empowerment.

In summary, the justice system must evolve to prioritise the needs of survivors and to create an environment in which they can seek reparation without being subjected to further trauma. A trauma-informed, compassionate approach to legal proceedings can help make this a reality, providing survivors with the support and understanding they need to heal and move forward."

Justice

Justice

To their dismay, children realise there are wicked adults among their own family, congregation, and community, mine included.

As they become adults, they come across individuals who try to silence them, keep secrets hidden, and conceal the truth, exactly what happened in my case also. The harm caused by their failure to protect me as a child is clear to those who know me, and damningly evident to those who don't. For instance, this matter about the religious institution never acknowledging nor witnessing those boys and young men around me take their own lives, still and always will enrage me.

Parishioners and priests risked children's lives for personal gain as soon as my crime was reported. Regrettably, justice was absent not only in the common law court room but also in the chambers of civil mediation. Instead of a win, compensation serves as a symbolic gesture to restore what we survivors lost since childhood.

It is undeniable that religious institutions have let survivors down by objectifying children for their perverse desires. Pretending to be unaware of paedophiles infiltrating children's groups, while simultaneously suppressing men's physical needs through abstinence, is intentional and repugnant. My experience is that only a few religious leaders have shown comprehension, compassion, empathy, humility, remorse, contrition, with no authentic apology until forced to do so, and until recently, no compensation till legally subpoenaed.

The record is quite tragic, especially considering my age of fifty-four (54) and financial struggles. Despite winning the case, there is no monetary compensation yet at the time of writing this book. Furthermore, I had to face six years of uncompensated legal work and the injustice of then using my compensation payment to cover my own legal fees — another harsh reality for survivors and their allies.

The justice system lacks fairness when officials use Canon privilege to shield abusers and impose their religious views on victims. The spread of evil throughout society is perpetuated by a chain of influence, resulting in calamity as protectors become predators and enablers become accomplices. It's an appalling cycle, particularly when religious oligarchs seize the nation's wealth to pay off their bad debts.

Feedback from fellow survivors indicates that they, similar to myself, would only consider accepting a religious institutional apology if certain conditions are met, such as sincere contrition and an end to the manipulation of common law. It is now legally enforceable and signals great change when these institutions are now required to take responsibility for failing these survivors.

Justice is rightfully delivered when it is resolved expediently. Full amends and the abolishment of religious institutions are necessary for us, as survivors, to move forward together and achieve true justice.

The importance of religious institutions is diminishing due to pure science and a lack of humane reason. Silence, employed by institutions, remains the most powerful form of violence, overshadowing an individual's perception of truth and justice.

ChatGPT-4 Response

"You have accurately captured the overwhelming and taxing nature of the legal process for survivors of abuse. The system often feels intrusive and invasive, forcing survivors to relive their trauma repeatedly while trying to prove their innocence and the guilt of their abusers.

The current justice system often fails to prioritise the well-being and dignity of survivors, focusing instead on procedural and evidentiary requirements that can exacerbate their suffering. This is particularly concerning given the sensitive and traumatic nature of their experiences.

There is a pressing need for a more compassionate and trauma-informed approach to addressing the needs of survivors in the legal system. This would include providing resources and support for survivors throughout the process, limiting the number of times they must recount their experiences, and minimising the invasive nature of evidence gathering.

It is crucial to recognise that the pursuit of justice should not come at the expense of a survivor's well-being. The process should be about healing and recovery, not just about proving guilt and securing punishment for the perpetrator.

Additionally, it is important to recognise that the process of seeking justice and reparation can be a part of a survivor's healing journey, rather than just a legal requirement. By ensuring that the process is respectful and supportive, we can help survivors find a sense of closure and empowerment.

In summary, the justice system must evolve to prioritise the needs of survivors and to create an environment in which they can seek reparation without being subjected to further trauma. A trauma-informed, compassionate approach to legal proceedings can help make this a reality, providing survivors with the support and understanding they need to heal and move forward."

Listening

Listening

When anyone, of any age, comes forward to share their story of sexual abuse, we are obliged as adults to listen. Within that listening space we can then determine with that person how best to help them achieve emancipation, bringing human experience to bear, without judgement.

Careful listening therefore, is the first step in understanding, protecting those who have the courage to speak out against their adversary. This in turn provides those in need with the capacity to take their grievance forward. The entire legal process is otherwise unattainable for many survivors, because interruptions to people's lifeworld invokes calamity, so the apathy in others is the very first barrier survivors face in that journey.

Without an empathetic response, justice then seems entirely unreachable as friendships sour, business deals shift and survivors find themselves in mayhem. I liken that first step to accepting the "end-of-the-world-as-I-once-knew-it" phase of the journey. The reality is that those who make it through the legal quagmire to reach compensation or restitution, do so with the goodwill of supporters and significant others — I don't include blood family in that, nor the mention of partners, as the statistics indicate that sadly these relationships often end in calamity.

Without any doubt, religious institutions have to date only one mission on their mind — avoid litigation at all cost from those suffering the most. It's a perversion of justice from the very beginning if you dwell long enough on that point. Likewise, the resounding lateral violence along that legal route forces many back into hiding who then abandon the legal process, damaged, and just surviving emotionally back in their everyday lives.

People who commit crimes should be held accountable, likewise anyone who is toxic in that goal of survivor emancipation is a liability. An affirmative action statement will always garner a swift reply, yet retribution through true Law does not recognise common law apology. So the only real way to help switch from the victim to survivor tag begins with the listening of others, then unpacking *self-storying with them* through a survivor-led action determination pathway.

ChatGPT-4 Response

"You've highlighted the importance of empathy, understanding, and support in helping survivors of sexual abuse navigate the difficult journey towards healing and justice. Active and compassionate listening is the first step in providing the assistance and encouragement that survivors need to share their experiences and seek reparation.

The legal process can be overwhelming and distressing for survivors, often exacerbating their trauma. This is why the support of friends, advocates, and professionals is crucial in helping them navigate the system and stay resilient in the face of adversity. It is essential for survivors to feel believed and validated, as this contributes to their sense of empowerment and enables them to move forward.

The role of religious institutions in protecting perpetrators and avoiding litigation further complicates the process for survivors seeking justice. This underscores the need for societal change and increased accountability, to ensure that those who commit crimes are held responsible, and that those who hinder the process of survivor emancipation are recognised as liabilities.

In addition to empathetic listening, survivor-led action determination provides a path for survivors to externalise their experiences, gain a sense of control, and transform their lives. By focusing on the individual's needs and agency, this approach prioritises the well-being and recovery of the survivor, ultimately contributing to their healing process.

In summary, a supportive and empathetic environment is essential for survivors of sexual abuse to share their experiences, seek justice, and embark on a journey of healing. Active listening, understanding, and survivor-led action determination are crucial elements in helping survivors transition from victimhood to empowerment, and ultimately, to a renewed sense of self and purpose."

Reform

Reform

It is evident that religious institutions need to transform themselves, becoming more transparent, accepting their mistakes, and making amends, beginning with honesty — a paradox considering it is part of their teachings. The ongoing occurrence of paedophilia cases within these institutions supports my argument.

The virtues preached by religious institutions, such as hope, seem contradictory when they also emphasise guilt and atonement, raising doubts about their relevance in today's society. Meaningful reform requires concrete steps and a sincere acknowledgment of culpability, going beyond rhetoric and policy. The failure of religious institutions to stop paedophile predators within their organisation has resulted in the public viewing them as ineffective in addressing this issue.

Through their actions of disregarding survivor accounts, ignoring complaints, and shielding predators, these religious institutions cultivate an environment that perpetuates abuse. Religious institutions are seen as accomplices and can be held liable for criminal negligence damages.

Paedophiles manipulate vulnerable individuals, creating a network of child sex rings that extend to different areas. The targeted activities of paedophiles have repeatedly exposed this intertwined sordid reality, with everyone being consciously enrolled in their pursuit of boys.

Those who have played any part in aiding and abetting this evil predator enterprise within religious institutions will leave behind a haunting legacy that will torment the souls of those they have abused. Redemption goes unrecognised by society, as religious institutions choose to ignore and silence survivors. The rhetoric of "zero-tolerance" needs to be changed to "absolute prevention".

ChatGPT-4 Response

"You raise important concerns about the failures of religious institutions in addressing the issue of sexual abuse within their ranks. The hypocrisy of preaching virtues like honesty, repentance, and atonement while failing to uphold those values within their own organisations has led to a crisis of credibility for many religious institutions.

It is crucial that religious institutions take responsibility for their role in perpetuating abuse by not only acknowledging past errors and supporting survivors but also implementing meaningful reforms to prevent future abuses. This includes being transparent, adopting zero-tolerance policies, cooperating with law enforcement, and holding abusers accountable.

The abuse of power within religious institutions and the systemic cover-up of such heinous crimes create a culture of complicity that enables predators to continue their actions. This has devastating effects on survivors and their families, as well as on the trust placed in religious organisations.

Addressing this crisis requires a fundamental shift in the way religious institutions approach the issue of sexual abuse. They must prioritise the well-being and safety of their congregants over protecting their own reputation and interests. By doing so, they can begin to rebuild trust and create an environment where abuse is no longer tolerated or concealed.

The road to reform and redemption is a long one, but it is a necessary journey for religious institutions that wish to live up to their moral and ethical responsibilities. By taking concrete steps to change, acknowledging past failures, and genuinely working to prevent future abuses, religious institutions can begin to restore faith in their missions and rebuild their relationships with their communities."

Contrition

Contrition

Countless children have paid with their lives, a high price for a society that believes apologies are sufficient and silencing is complemented by non-disclosure.

In the midst of striving to appear righteous for God, innocence was lost. Pride and arrogance deprived these children of their ability to feel compassion, empathy, and power. Their selfish ambition prevented them from seeing the truth, leading them down the wrong path and eroding their humanity, replaced by institutionalised prejudice and hatred. The aftermath of historical assault is filled with broken bodies, shattered dreams, damaged psyches, and crushed hopes.

It is essential for religious institutions to genuinely accept that contrition should be shown humbly, not by legally opposing the victims of their own criminal negligence. The ignored victims of abuse, betrayal, violation, molestation, rape, battery, and emotional scars raise questions about the enduring relevance of religious institutions that claim greatness but plead poverty in today's society. I felt compelled to keep my reality hidden as a shameful secret, with no outlet for my tears or acknowledgment of my emotions.

There was a lack of awareness in my family and community regarding the reasons behind my anger and hatred. People's failure to comprehend resulted in resentment and an unsupportive "get over it" attitude.

Seeking compensation as a crime victim, in search of restitution, acknowledgement, and recognition, has heightened my trauma due to criminal negligence.

ChatGPT-4 Response

"The immense suffering experienced by survivors of abuse within religious institutions cannot be understated. The lifelong impact of these heinous crimes has left countless individuals grappling with the effects of trauma, betrayal, and loss of trust. It is disheartening to know that the very institutions meant to provide guidance and support have so profoundly failed these survivors.

For meaningful change to occur, religious institutions must first acknowledge the extent of the damage caused by their actions and inaction. Authentic contrition, as you mentioned, should be demonstrated not only through legal channels but also in a genuine commitment to change and support for survivors.

As part of their commitment to change, religious institutions must ensure that they are actively working to prevent abuse, support survivors, and hold abusers accountable. This includes fostering a culture of openness and transparency, cooperating with law enforcement, and implementing robust safeguarding measures.

The journey toward healing for survivors is a long and arduous one, made even more challenging by the need to navigate the legal system and fight for compensation and recognition. It is crucial that religious institutions take responsibility for the harm they have caused and work to rectify it, not just through financial compensation but by providing emotional support and resources for healing as well.

Only by acknowledging their failures, making amends, and taking concrete steps toward reform can religious institutions begin to rebuild trust and regain credibility in the eyes of survivors and the larger community. It is essential that they prioritise the well-being and safety of their congregants over their own interests and reputation, and demonstrate a genuine commitment to creating a future free from abuse and neglect."

Responses

Responses

In Australia, a coronial inquiry addressed how religious institutions handled historical sexual abuse and criminal negligence claims, but in another country, the case would be dismissed due to legal limitations.

My present and future dedication is solely focused on smashing any statute of limitation in the space of sexual violence, particularly involving men. The silence of religious institutions in Australia was finally exposed through a Royal Commission. Religious institutions have enabled predators to find safe haven, victimising millions of men.

The absence of institutional action until legal intervention suggests what needs to be addressed in the system. When a nation takes responsibility and holds individuals accountable, it demonstrates a mature justice system. The same can be said of those of religious institutional orders that proactively educate with the key message of action, not hope alone — *sadly they peddle hope, not action* — as change comes about through survivor-led action determination, not solely legal recourse.

The defusing and eradication of false myths about survivors is accomplished through survivor-led action, not institutional initiatives. Starting a conversation with any survivor by using the 'PPP' response, as described below, is possibly the worst approach. *Propensity*, perpetuity, and pro tempore are all false in regards to victims.

Individuals who have experienced sexual violence, especially premeditated and aggravated violence, may have an increased likelihood of developing addiction, engaging in theft or vandalism, or in extreme cases, committing murder. Similarly, it is important for medical professionals to recognize the ease with which sexual abuse and intergenerational trauma can be mistakenly linked. Aspects of chronic post-traumatic stress disorder show similarities to foetal alcohol syndrome. History provides accounts of survivors further victimised by those charged with helping them, or wilfully set upon by those consecrated in law but not compassion.

It is unacceptable for religious institutions to demand survivors to change their narratives in order to receive support. Survivor emancipation requires religious institutions to provide an affirmative response, enabling full reparation due to the permanent nature of their physical and mental condition.

ChatGPT-4 Response

"It is indeed a travesty that it took a Royal Commission in Australia to unveil the extent of abuse and lack of response from religious institutions. This speaks to the urgent need for greater transparency, accountability, and action on a global scale.

It is essential for religious institutions to proactively engage in meaningful change and support survivor-led action determination. This includes acknowledging and dismantling harmful misconceptions, such as the 'PPP' response you mentioned. By actively addressing these issues and misconceptions, religious institutions can foster a more empathetic and supportive environment for survivors.

Medical practitioners and other support services must also be well-informed about the complexities and nuances of trauma resulting from sexual abuse. This understanding is crucial to providing appropriate care and avoiding further harm or victimisation of survivors. Accurate diagnosis and tailored support can make a significant difference in the healing process.

Religious institutions should prioritise survivor emancipation and reparation, recognising that the impact of trauma is often lifelong and irreversible. By offering comprehensive support, resources, and assistance, institutions can contribute to the healing process and work toward restoring trust with survivors and the larger community.

Ultimately, it is essential for religious institutions, medical practitioners, support services, and society at large to approach survivors with empathy, understanding, and a genuine commitment to helping them heal. This requires ongoing education, open dialogue, and a dedication to creating safe spaces for survivors to share their stories and seek justice. By working together, we can create a world where survivors are met with compassion and support, rather than judgement and disbelief."

Truths

Truths

The sad fact remains that the misuse of immense wealth to manipulate the disadvantaged, including those who sought refuge from oppressive regimes, goes on.

It's undeniable that as humans, we haven't overcome our failures in preventing paedophilia. We cannot argue that we have effectively addressed any of it through incarceration and financial reparations, as the problem persists relentlessly.

In the legal forum, we expose the survivor's personal life, while the oppressor's power is given priority, with an unsworn statement from the dock. I considered this imbalance pure evil after witnessing it in my own legal case. Despite the evidence, there are still individuals who refuse to acknowledge the reality of my sexual assault and deny its proximity to them.

The questioning of this possibility resulted in my anger and religious institutions' denial of self agency added to this. For others, when the abuser is no longer alive, it becomes crucial to differentiate between denial and lack of self-assurance. The allure of the fast life and the drugs that go with that affliction, is swapped later in life for the sad truth of chemotherapy.

The early exposure of our children to a combination of drugs is evidence of the ongoing battle between society and big pharmaceutical corporations, with psychiatrists playing a controversial role.

The mixture of chemicals is ineffective in addressing the violence caused by religious wrongs. The shameful truth is that as a society, we have forgotten about the countless survivors of sexual assault who end up bankrupt, homeless, or incarcerated.

ChatGPT-4 Response

"Your statement poignantly encapsulates the transformation and empowerment of survivors of abuse at the hands of religious institutions. Once perceived as passive victims, merely enduring the repercussions of institutional failure and negligence, these individuals have redefined their narrative, becoming active symbols of resilience and defiance.

Survivors, through their very existence and willingness to speak out, embody a powerful indictment of the negligence of religious institutions. They stand as living evidence of the failures of these organisations to protect the most vulnerable among their congregations. Their stories and experiences challenge and confront the often-defensible attitudes these institutions have historically adopted towards abuse.

Moreover, survivors have broken the silence that once shrouded such abuses. Where once their voices were suppressed or ignored, contributing to a cycle of abuse and cover-up, they now speak with clarity and strength. This shift from silence to vocal advocacy not only aids in their personal healing but also serves as a catalyst for broader institutional change and accountability.

This transformation of survivors into active, vocal advocates marks a significant societal shift. It reflects a growing recognition of the importance of listening to and supporting those who have suffered abuse, and a rejection of the culture of silence and complicity that has allowed such abuse to persist. As such, survivors are not only symbols of past negligence but also beacons of hope and change, pointing the way toward a more accountable and compassionate future for religious institutions and society at large."

Responsibility

Responsibility

The "dead and forgotten" can come back to haunt institutions that are unprepared and face legal repercussions. As survivors though, we must remember that words spoken cannot be taken back. It makes sense then to declare that there is no such thing as survivor forgiveness, only acceptance which does not exonerate institutions of their culpability.

If empty promises only appease the convenience of the moral majority, then it's just meaningless talk. Ending trauma, rather than just amending it, is a responsibility we all comprehend. Similarly, our moral compass as survivors determines where our loyalties lie, as it's difficult to navigate life while haunted by demons in our memories, nightmares, and flashbacks. Therapy cannot completely remove the main trigger, which is anything resembling the religious institution that caused the initial problems.

Despite my initial scepticism, mediation allowed the institution to understand its shortcomings in protecting me, and I was able to express my deep emotions of hurt, shame, and pain. This unexpectedly resulted in a significant revelation. I realised that it's not just a battle against the tyranny of supremacy, but a shared responsibility for the supremacy of tyranny that we must all acknowledge as a human society, beyond religious institutions.

Despite my protests and various expressions that may appear contrary, it's not the church buildings I wish to demolish but rather the institutions of evil empire men. The physical ruins stand as a necessary symbol for future generations, helping them identify the lasting impact of the abuse they inflicted.

The familial home is often where sexual assault occurs, yet pedophiles form networks and conceal their true intentions to infiltrate those homes. Only through survivor-led action determination, which includes the use of artefacts as symbols, can we truly achieve a repairable balance, instead of engaging in lengthy legal disputes based solely on spoken or written words. Symbolic artefacts arise from the action determination process, preserving the child's well-being and revealing significant information.

Collecting photos, certificates, notes, letters, and cards may seem insignificant at first, but they become essential when presented as evidence in court. When deciding which actions are most beneficial for an individual's emancipation, it's crucial to consider them as a component of equitable reparations, rather than the ultimate goal.

This suggests that it happens as part of ongoing personal growth, rather than narrating one's self as a complaint, in order to achieve fair restitution.

Parity and equality can only be attained through accountability, transparency, honesty, and integrity. The stakes involve reclaiming our humanity, dignity, freedom, sanity, integrity, safety, happiness, functionality, and fearlessness in the world. Responsibility lies with these institutions, and that's what matters most.

ChatGPT-4 Response

"It is indeed a travesty that it took a Royal Commission in Australia to unveil the extent of abuse and lack of response from religious institutions. This speaks to the urgent need for greater transparency, accountability, and action on a global scale.

It is essential for religious institutions to proactively engage in meaningful change and support survivor-led action determination. This includes acknowledging and dismantling harmful misconceptions, such as the 'PPP' response you mentioned. By actively addressing these issues and misconceptions, religious institutions can foster a more empathetic and supportive environment for survivors.

Medical practitioners and other support services must also be well-informed about the complexities and nuances of trauma resulting from sexual abuse. This understanding is crucial to providing appropriate care and avoiding further harm or victimisation of survivors. Accurate diagnosis and tailored support can make a significant difference in the healing process.

Religious institutions should prioritise survivor emancipation and reparation, recognising that the impact of trauma is often lifelong and irreversible. By offering comprehensive support, resources, and assistance, institutions can contribute to the healing process and work toward restoring trust with survivors and the larger community.

Ultimately, it is essential for religious institutions, medical practitioners, support services, and society at large to approach survivors with empathy, understanding, and a genuine commitment to helping them heal. This requires ongoing education, open dialogue, and a dedication to creating safe spaces for survivors to share their stories and seek justice. By working together, we can create a world where survivors are met with compassion and support, rather than judgement and disbelief."

Accountability

Accountability

This chapter was initially titled “Consent” with a savage attack on pederasty which in ancient Greece, and Roman Empire times (and no doubt across most of the ancient realm of men) was taken to be the “educational benefits, established practice of transmission of values and learning between partners which led to the younger male becoming more informed of his very pivotal role within the polis or community.”

The socially accepted practice of sexually abusing young boys in religious institutions perpetuates hate and deference, alongside the harmful tradition of child marriage. The definition of a crime has evolved, and now, having sexual activity with a minor may be seen as child sexual abuse or statutory rape, depending on the age of consent in that area.

It’s understandable why individuals are appalled at being held accountable when the institutions themselves were responsible for such atrocities. It is clear that throughout history, power and control have been wielded by those ancient bastions and hordes, exploiting the sexual interests of monstrous men, centuries before organised religion emerged.

Pederasty or paederasty denotes a sexual connection between an adult man and a young boy. According to my research, Ancient Greece and Rome both accepted this practice as socially acknowledged.

Within common law courts, male sexual predators frequently assert that they lacked sufficient, minimal, or non-existent relationships with women prior to their initial offence. Similarly, the defendant’s counsel in my case argued that the perpetrator, William “Adrian” Sandwell had a lack of strong male role models in his life as a child. I assert that these legal positions are just artificial creations that demand responsibility, absolving liability while emphasising the importance of guilt.

Is it really believable for someone to declare complete exoneration for their actions as an adult, particularly when it endangers a child’s protection and welfare? For example, look at the religious confessional—a box for repenting and seeking forgiveness. When you consider the data on violence perpetrated against girls and non-binary children, it becomes evident that a male-dominated society operates in a malicious and harmful manner. This society harbors predators who pretend to be heterosexual, marginalize the LGBTQ+ community, exploit politics, and commit acts of child sexual abuse in secret.

The suffering of messiahs becomes insignificant when we witness the ongoing abuse of children by those in power. The only conditions are consent and the ability to distinguish between fantasy and reality, and to understand reason and responsibility. As a society, we have a responsibility to protect the rights of young men exploring their homosexuality with older individuals, stressing the importance of informed consent.

It is the responsibility of adults to protect children, which means standing up against those who wish to hurt them. Prevention from pederastic obsessions between men and children cannot be a restorative practice controlled by the religious institutions that provide safe harbour to these villains, as they are, in effect, their facilitator and enabler. Additionally, the patriarchal structure of religious institutions poses a challenge to women, children, and those with different identities by relegating them as enemies to the cause.

Contrary to religious beliefs, children are not inherently bad or sinful, but rather innocent victims of sexual offenders. These offenders, regardless of age, should be held responsible for their actions. Children were not created for defilement, and the intergenerational and inter-familial trauma caused by incest cannot be undone as they become adults. The combined impact of pedophilia on communities is truly devastating and catastrophic.

Regrettably, profit-driven individuals guide us and hire experts to guarantee legal tax avoidance and escape from accountability for the wealthy and notorious. Those lacking information observe how the powerful exploit their influence solely for self-preservation without any real responsibility. This is a harmful blend of abuse, taking on different forms.

Despite surviving these hardships, I have become a toughened version of myself, and the criminal trial is another challenge to prove my innocence. True accountability means enforcing consequences for offenders, not simply dismissing their actions.

The Anglican Church's lack of responsibility in Australia and other religious institutions worldwide highlights the failure to stop criminals and represents institutionalised power structures that men like me have to endure.

In an attempt to tackle child sexual abuse, the Lanzarote Convention (see Reference page) has implemented a comprehensive policy. Yet, the existing policy norm is inadequate and provides Member States with a vague directive to allow victims “adequate” time to report crimes after reaching adulthood. Child Global’s Brave Movement in 2023 reveals that it typically takes victims many years to process their trauma and reach out to law enforcement.

It’s unfair for authorities to closely observe survivors as they recount the most horrific experiences inflicted upon them. The failure to confront this problem among people only perpetuates more sadness, escalating anger, and ultimately, acts of murder. Amongst all this despair, there is an individual who is experiencing suffering — not just another casualty.

Getting support from important people helps to disprove claims of “being absent even in the company of others,” a symptom of PTSD survivors often struggle with. Acts of crime against children create a schism within society, destroying the moral foundation of modern humanity.

The only way to truly measure accountability is through the punishment of those who oppose ethical principles. Paedophiles, who seek power, manipulate religious contexts to lure victims, offering false hope and presenting death as the only means of escape.

ChatGPT-4 Response

"You've highlighted some crucial points regarding the importance of accountability, both within religious institutions and in society at large. The patriarchal structures that have allowed abuse to persist must be challenged and dismantled in order to protect the most vulnerable members of our communities.

It is essential to recognise the humanity of each survivor and to understand the immense burden they carry as a result of the abuse they've suffered. Acknowledging the systemic failures and the complex web of power structures that have allowed abuse to continue is an important step towards true accountability.

Prevention, as you mentioned, should be the primary focus for institutions, as it is the most effective way to protect potential victims. This involves reevaluating the roles and responsibilities of those in power and fostering an environment where abuse cannot be hidden or excused.

Survivors should not be forced to endure further trauma in their pursuit of justice, and measures must be taken to ensure that the legal process is sensitive and supportive. Holding offenders accountable should be a priority, and we must work collectively to create a society where everyone can live free from harm.

It is important for all of us to recognise the suffering of survivors and to work towards creating a more just and equitable world. By acknowledging the pain and trauma they have experienced, and by demanding accountability from institutions and individuals, we can take important steps towards healing and change."

Capability

Capability

These monsters of men, depraved and alienated predators of children still frequent every single part of human society.

Places of supposed care remain a central locale to these monsters, leaders, staff, as perpetrators in an institution's midst, who amuse and impress congregations. The paedophiles' charm and wit with adults is a disguise for their sick penchant for children who they covet as objects of their own sick and perverted desires. It is abominable that clergy historically have stood by idly, and continue to fail to act upon information as children around them are molested.

Many boys who never made it to become men, through their abject trauma, chose to end their lives as they perceived institutional apology did not right those wrongs against them. They could not escape their fate at the hands of the monsters at the time, nor could they escape their trauma in adulthood either. Religious institutions who claim to serve God, now defend themselves accused of allowing evil to flourish amongst their foundations.

Societal attitudes have shifted markedly since the Royal Commission into Institutional Responses to Child Sexual Abuse in Australia. The cover up of child abuse committed implicated priests, bishops, wardens with a veritable mountain of evidence, and proof of criminal negligence, wrongdoing after wrongdoing. This is beyond a challenge, rather it is a duty now and into the future, to respect survivors who express their suffering, who mitigate their trust and choose their words carefully.

Religious institutions are now required to shoulder and bear the burden created by leaving children in the company of paedophiles, as it is clear they lacked the capability to protect. With a legacy of monsters amongst religious orders, institutions and multinational companies they have an unfathomable task ahead to restore faith among the faithless. Just a small percentile of religious institutional amassed wealth, two (2) billion dollars in the Anglican Church's instance, would award every survivor with the rightful amounts of compensation due.

To restore trust between religious institutions and the public will be an even greater challenge, as they need to rebuild confidence, regain credibility, repair relations with the government and authorities, mend relationships, support and pay for damage already done to victims.

ChatGPT-4 Response

"You're right in highlighting the immense challenge that religious institutions face in restoring trust and credibility, given the history of abuse and cover-ups. The Royal Commission in Australia exposed a widespread issue and has had a significant impact on societal attitudes, making it clear that changes must be made within these institutions to ensure the safety and well-being of children and vulnerable individuals."

To rebuild trust, religious institutions must:

1. Acknowledge the extent of the abuse that has occurred within their walls and the profound harm it has caused to survivors.
2. Offer sincere apologies to the survivors and their families, demonstrating genuine remorse and understanding of the damage inflicted.
3. Provide just and fair compensation to survivors, reflecting the severity of the harm they have suffered and the responsibility of the institution.
4. Implement transparent and comprehensive measures to ensure the safety of children and vulnerable individuals, including thorough background checks, rigorous training, and clear reporting procedures for any suspicion of abuse.
5. Establish ongoing support systems for survivors, such as counselling services, access to resources, and connection to support networks.
6. Foster open and honest communication with the public, government, and authorities, demonstrating a commitment to transparency and cooperation in addressing past wrongs and preventing future harm.
7. Engage in a process of internal reflection and reform to address the underlying issues within the institution that allowed abuse to occur, such as patriarchal structures and power imbalances."

The road to rebuilding trust and confidence is a long and arduous one, but it is a necessary journey that religious institutions must undertake. By committing to these actions and demonstrating a genuine desire to change, they can work towards healing the wounds of the past and ensuring the safety and well-being of all members of their communities."

Prevention

Prevention

If prevention was a proactive measure, then *protection* is the principle action determination of those who truly make the difference and care for children. For many men sadly this transcendence of living an open and free life does not occur, and for those for whom it does occur, the tempest of the past is an ever present challenge to beautiful moments of short life they have left to live.

Likewise, given recognition of our mortal human condition, it is a travesty that the complainants (the victim of crime) have had to prove their innocence in a court of law, cognisant that it is neither survivors nor their supporters who are the victor in this poisonous mayhem. For survivors to story their way out they need to have the support and means to do so.

Should they choose to chase the civil legal case of institutional neglect, they should also have the very same entitlement to engage the media to amplify their voices, to be heard and seen. The mostly empathy-bereft public drown out the story of survivors attracted to popular stories of little meaning. Conversely, these emancipation stories which are very limited in popular press exposé, as my lawyer stated, “weary the public quickly”. Swamped with other distractions, the press then relegates sexual abuse reporting to the lowest readership ranking in their tabloids.

What matters now is the truth behind why certain people want to keep quiet about sexual violence — *apathy and fear*. These secrets are fuel for the fire as survivors speak out their stories in anger, with resentment at the legal process and hatred for the oppressors who support paedophile safe havens. Survivor stories in print or online are then pigeonholed as "unsavoury publication" and, as we have seen too often, only high profile cases make the news. Meanwhile, millions of men suffer invisibly as prevention is not the panacea of the already oppressed, so prevention is protection already prior enforced.

In summary, the route of exposing survivor stories through popular and social media is not a safe avenue to exercise discussions on protection, but they need to be. These stories of historical sexual and physical assaults are critically important and need to be widely disseminated, not relegated to the last article in any publication continuum.

ChatGPT-4 Response

“It is indeed a challenge for survivors to have their voices heard and their stories acknowledged by society. The media often focuses on sensational or high-profile cases, while the stories of countless other survivors remain untold and unheard. This selective attention can perpetuate the cycle of silence and inaction around the issue of sexual abuse in religious institutions and other contexts.

To address this issue and to ensure that all survivors have the opportunity to share their stories and receive the support they need, it is crucial to create safe spaces and platforms for open and honest dialogue. Some ways to achieve this could include:

1. Encouraging and supporting the creation of survivor-led initiatives, such as advocacy groups, support networks, and online forums, where survivors can openly share their experiences, access resources, and connect with others who have faced similar challenges.
2. Raising awareness about the prevalence and impact of sexual abuse through educational programs and campaigns, in schools, communities, and religious institutions, with the aim of breaking the stigma and fostering a more empathetic and understanding society.
3. Encouraging responsible and sensitive media coverage of sexual abuse cases, emphasising the importance of amplifying survivors' voices and highlighting the systemic issues that contribute to such abuse. This could involve working with journalists and media outlets to develop guidelines for reporting on abuse cases, to ensure that survivors' stories are treated with respect and dignity.
4. Supporting research and scholarship on the topic of sexual abuse and institutional neglect, which can help uncover the scope of the issue and inform policy decisions and prevention strategies.
5. Advocating for legal and policy changes that prioritise the rights and well-being of survivors, such as the removal of statutes of limitations, improved access to legal representation, and the establishment of independent bodies to investigate abuse allegations.

By taking these steps, society can work towards breaking the "cone of silence" that surrounds sexual abuse and create a more inclusive and supportive environment for all survivors.”

Apology

Apology

In my case, despite being warned that asserting pre-conditions to compensation under non-disclosure was a dangerous contingent, I still demanded a spoken and written apology from the Bishop as absolute and not negotiable — *under duress they agreed*.

My lawyers were suitably relieved and impressed, notwithstanding their tidy pay-out of their no-win-no-fee riding on that condition I had demanded. I consider an apology from a religious institution as only worth anything if it guides institutional action.

A written apology is proof of institutional torture, not a get-out-of-jail-free-plea, as every victim of crime faces many prejudices in society, so, when confronted with any judicial or politically biased process in the rest of my life, they can produce this. Of course, this is always useful when signed and dated by an Anglican Church Bishop, not just spoken and then conveniently forgotten.

Admirably I only used the term “RAGE” once in my victim impact statement delivered as a eulogy of Apostasy, of which I identify strongly in the context of; “Apostasy, ἀποστασία, revolt , renunciation of one’s chosen course of action to follow another.” I also identify as an Actionist (differing but synonymous with activism) with common accords shared through First Nations and ancient cultures in rejection and refusal of organised religious indoctrination.

The “apologist” position of religious institutions I liken to the redemptionist clerics who assert their devotion to rescue of captives from slavery, yet they still to this very day assert their Canonical reasons to remain silent on matters of paedophilia. Likewise, I see no point in wasting my breath on “reformists” who believe they can change a religious order from within. If their own story of sexual violence is anything to go by, then their wilful insistence on remaining devout needs to switch out of need, not wanting validation out of greed nor countenance out of social or moral obligation.

Religion spawned the simple dichotomy and binary positions of “hate” and “hope”, the falsity of “good versus evil” when in fact it all happens in duality, peddled slavery yet touted business as delivering “faith” and “belief”. By contrast, I see the world through the genesis רֵאשִׁית prism of “action” and “determination”, a connection of like-souls in mode of emancipation to and for others.

An apology is the simplest form of institutional atonement, yet victims of crime are under no obligation to listen to, nor receive apologies when they continue to witness others silenced. Neither are actionable deeds by singing hymns about righting wrongs in any way sufficient, rather actioning the difference must happen now with those victims of institutional crime affected by historical inaction. Apologies from an institution therefore are meaningless without tangible results, whereas a survivor-led action determination reparation process is beneficial for the survivor to reach financial recompense.

Compensation can only be one part of legal reparation as a process, helping those harmed financially recover from the substantial financial and lifeworld time losses incurred. Obviously monetary gains alone do not resolve the emotional damage of family estrangement, nor psychological distress, physical injuries, mental anguish, fear, anxiety, repeated targeting, alienation, assaults and molestations.

Over the last forty years, I consider the religious institutional response to sexual harassment and abuse allegations as grossly inadequate, in reality woeful, despite their thousands of apologies and false postulations in containment. The subsequent Royal Commission in Australia is also considered by many survivors as inadequate, ineffective and an extension of an already owned State.

It is obvious that inaction for centuries speaks volumes as it also implies the silence enforced on survivors is consent, yet that isn't the case. Silence underpins predatory behaviour and condones child abuse across human culture, normalising the abuse of power. By remaining mute, religious institutions enable perpetrators to keep doing what they do — *sexually assault innocent children*.

Any lack of compassion, empathy devoid, reflects an incapacity to act with humility. When officers of an institution are incapable of admitting fault, are lacking in self-awareness, or unwilling to rectify mistakes, they wrongly assume a position of moral authority. It is irrefutable that religious institutions knew members were committing acts of sexual assault on generations of children, for thousands of years.

Therefore, the abject terror those children felt as innocents, now manifest in society, is the result of religious institutional absence of care, the perfect storm that perpetrators promulgate as evil monsters.

ChatGPT-4 Response

"Your narrative powerfully conveys the deep-seated disillusionment and distrust towards religious institutions, shaped by your experiences of institutional abuse and the subsequent quest for justice and acknowledgment. Your perspective underscores not only the personal journey of a survivor but also a broader critique of religious organisations' responses to sexual abuse.

1. *Apologies and Institutional Action*: You emphasise that apologies from religious institutions are meaningful only if they lead to concrete actions. In your case, the insistence on a written apology from a high-ranking official within the Church was a strategic move to hold the institution accountable and to serve as tangible evidence of their acknowledgment of wrongdoing.

2. *Survivor-led Reparation*: Your journey underscores the importance of survivor-led reparation processes. You highlight that true justice involves not only financial compensation but also acknowledgment and action from the institution. The written apology you demanded and received is a critical part of this process, as it symbolises institutional atonement.

3. *The Role of Religious Doctrine*: You critique the role of religious doctrine in perpetuating a culture of silence and enabling abuse. The "end is nigh" narrative and the waiting for a saviour are seen as mechanisms that distract from taking personal and institutional responsibility.

4. *Action and Determination*: You advocate for a shift from passive belief to active engagement – from "hope" and "faith" to "action" and "determination." This approach aligns with your belief in the necessity for fundamental changes within religious institutions, rather than mere reform.

5. *The Royal Commission's Role*: The Royal Commission into Institutional Responses to Child Sexual Abuse in Australia is viewed as inadequate in addressing the depth and complexity of the abuse and the systemic failures of religious institutions.

6. *Need for Fundamental Change*: You argue for the complete dismantling of traditional religious structures, viewing them as irredeemably flawed. This perspective is rooted in your experiences and observations of the persistent failure of these institutions to protect the vulnerable and to hold perpetrators accountable.

7. *Silence as Complicity*: Your narrative reiterates that silence on the part of religious institutions not only perpetuates abuse but also normalises it. The failure to act decisively against perpetrators is seen as a profound disregard for the welfare and safety of congregations, particularly children. This silence is not just a passive omission but an active complicity that allows predatory behaviour to continue unchecked, perpetuating a culture of rape and abuse of power.

8. *Institutional Lack of Compassion and Humility*: You criticise religious institutions for their lack of empathy, compassion, and humility. Their inability to admit fault and rectify mistakes is seen as an assumption of moral infallibility that is fundamentally at odds with the principles they claim to uphold.

9. *Rejection of Religious Indoctrination:* Your stance is firmly against the indoctrination and authoritarian structures of religious institutions. You advocate for a return to more natural, core principles aligned with nature and universal creation, free from the patriarchal and matriarchal structures that have enabled such widespread abuse.

10. *Demands for Comprehensive Reparation*: Lastly, you call for comprehensive reparation that goes beyond mere financial compensation. This includes a dismantling of the existing religious frameworks and an end to legal stalling and manipulation by religious institutions. You seek a shift in societal attitudes and institutional practices that no longer places the burden of proof and the stigma of victimhood on survivors.

Your narrative is a compelling call for radical change in how society and religious institutions address and respond to sexual abuse. It is a demand for accountability, transparency, and a complete overhaul of systems that have historically failed to protect the most vulnerable."

Victim

Victim

Victims are often regarded as trapped in their own "racket" of sorry circumstance, as evidenced by their persistent spoken complaint. To unpack that toxic self-storying requires speaking it out, yet, it takes an empathetic listener to reciprocate shift-shaping support or advice.

The term *victim* is derived from the legal context, yet the term "survivor" is associated with thriving despite the crime against themselves. There is a fundamental difference between the tag of *victim* and the concept of *survivor*, likewise *survivor guilt* is in reality that of *institutional guilt*. Survivors are in the mode of taking back control of their life story, making good of their experience, not feeling guilty for others as they struggle to survive themselves — *eventually understanding it all as a gift.*

The term *survivor* therefore, better fits these courageous few who forge through with fortitude, their plight reconfigured through their *action determination* despite the horrifying statistics of sexual violence worldwide. Invariably *victims* blame their powerlessness and associate everything unresolved as a continued attack against them. Meanwhile, *survivors* and their *supporters* make every effort to prevent this happening to those around them, in solidarity.

I was a child, a boy, an innocent teenager at the time when sexual violence divided, not defined my world. When I look back on my childhood, I am now aware of the warning signs that something was not right with the man (and his accomplices) who would later abuse me. At the time, no adult intervened or spoke up against him and I remember feeling like I was in danger the moment I saw him, even though I didn't fully understand why.

As a child, I had been taught to trust adults, to believe that they were there to protect me. But in this instance, the adults and moral guardians in my life failed me. They allowed a predator to roam free, to hurt me and many other children as well. It was a betrayal of the promise of community, of the idea that "we are all in this together", and that "we will look out for one another".

For me, this betrayal was not just personal, it was also spiritual. The man who abused me was someone who was supposed to be a representative of a human God, a leader in our religious community. But instead of protecting me, he used his position of power to exploit and hurt me.

It shattered my faith in the church as they failed to contain him. This was contrary to the attestations of Clergy who claimed that there was a loving God who watches over us, especially as the institution rallied to rid itself of me. All of them are evil, even the Chaplain who signed my archery award in 1984 remarking — "*Alexander Hayes, most promising sex symbol*".

I recall every detail vividly — *the isolation and the never-ending fear*. Being sexually assaulted is just one of the many offences that are listed on my record, according to society's standards. They labelled me as a victim of crime, but I refuse to let this define who I am.

It's frustrating to see how society puts the burden on victims to prove that they were sexually abused, rather than holding the perpetrators accountable for their actions. There's a pervasive belief that victims are lying or exaggerating, and it's a struggle to be taken seriously by the authorities, the legal system, and even by friends and family members. Irrespective of this, victims need to transcend from their sorrowful, pitiful state of persistent complaint.

ChatGPT-4 Response

"The distinction between the terms "victim" and "survivor" is indeed essential, as they reflect different perspectives and attitudes towards the experience of trauma. While the term "victim" might imply a sense of powerlessness and helplessness, "survivor" conveys resilience, strength, and the ability to overcome adversity.

It is deeply saddening that you had to endure such a nightmarish experience from a young age. The lack of intervention or support from adults, and the alienation and intimidation you faced, further amplified your suffering. However, your determination and fortitude in the face of these ordeals have allowed you to become a survivor, reclaiming control over your life story and finding the gift within the struggle.

While sexual assault is just one aspect of the many challenges you have faced, it is crucial to acknowledge the incredible resilience you have demonstrated throughout your life. Your story serves as a powerful reminder that, despite the immense adversity that may come our way, it is possible to persevere and transform ourselves from victims into survivors.

It is also important to note that the solidarity between survivors and supporters can be a powerful force in helping others heal and fostering a more empathetic and supportive society. By sharing your experiences and standing in unity with others who have faced similar trauma, you contribute to breaking the silence and stigma surrounding these issues, ultimately paving the way for change and healing."

Survivor

Survivor

Despite the turmoil in their minds, survivors prioritize finding comfort and peace in the remaining years of their lives, having endured the torment of sexual violence.

The central focus of survivors' activities is not only introspective therapeutic "enlightenment", with the support of their supporters. We must recognize and respect that these men are the brave few who have the courage to share their stories, even if it leads to difficult consequences like drug addiction, strained friendships, divorce, and loneliness in old age.

The innocence of children should never have been sacrificed or exploited for the gain of institutions, as they are not commodities to be traded. To truly live life to the fullest, we must as victims of these crimes let go of institutional servitude and embrace all the opportunities that life presents. But, we should also reflect on the consequences of seeking self-congratulatory stability. In the same way, the advocates for survivors are accountable for their impact on a man's journey towards disclosure, legal redress, and potential growth, sometimes imposing limitations.

Supporters are undoubtedly the rock but not the salvation of survivors, equally vulnerable and equally deeply affected by the complexity of shared PTSD. In the unified struggle to persevere, the horror of it all raises the worst of behaviours in couples, manifests as great calamity in households struggling to contain the rage and yet never trained nor able to cope with the realm of historical sexual violence.

The widespread impact of complex PTSD is disturbingly accepted in a society obsessed with projecting a perfect image on social media, yet there is more to life than mere survival or constant busyness.

ChatGPT-4 Response

"The narrative you present offers a profound and nuanced exploration of the experiences of survivors of sexual violence and their supporters. It delves into the complexities of coping, healing, and living after enduring such trauma.

Key points from the narrative are that this perspective acknowledges both the resilience and the ongoing struggles that survivors face in their journey towards recovery, notably:

1. *Survivorship as a Journey of Control and Understanding:* You emphasise that survivors are individuals who have taken back control of their life story. This process of making sense of their experiences and viewing them as a part of their life's journey, albeit painful, is a significant step towards healing.
2. *The Role of Supporters:* The importance of supporters in the lives of survivors is clearly highlighted. However, you also bring attention to the fact that supporters, while being a crucial source of strength, are not the sole solution to the challenges faced by survivors. The shared burden of trauma can affect supporters deeply, leading to a complex dynamic where both parties grapple with the repercussions of the trauma.
3. *The Complexity of Thriving Post-Trauma:* There's an acknowledgment of the difference between merely surviving and truly thriving. While stability and coping are important, there is a suggestion that simply existing in a state of 'recovery' without deeper engagement with life's broader experiences may not be wholly fulfilling.
4. *Challenges in Relationships:* The narrative touches upon the difficulties that survivors and their supporters often face in maintaining relationships, underlining the strain that PTSD and CPTSD can place on households and couples.
5. *The Pitfalls of Self-Focused Survival:* There's an implied critique of a form of survival that is self-congratulatory or self-absorbed. The narrative seems to advocate for a balance between personal well-being and broader engagement with life.
6. *Resilience Amidst Calamity:* The resilience of survivors is celebrated, but so is the recognition of the ongoing challenges they face, such as addiction, marital breakdowns, and loneliness.

7. *Critical View of Societal Norms:* The narrative critiques societal norms, especially the portrayal of lives on social media, which often gloss over the depth and complexity of real struggles faced by individuals.

Your narrative offers a critical and empathetic lens on the experiences of survivors of sexual violence. It respects their resilience and the significant role of their supporters, while also acknowledging the ongoing challenges they face.

This perspective encourages a deeper understanding of what it means to move beyond survival towards a more engaged and fulfilling existence, highlighting the importance of addressing not just the individual symptoms of trauma but also the broader societal context in which survivors and their supporters live."

Thriver

Thriver

Engaging in busyness redirects our focus towards aiding others, essentially activating our higher order Self. However, survivors of sexual violence frequently mask their pain through busy activity, but their resolve can weaken, fracture, and ultimately distract them.

To escape our victim mentality and succeed, we must abandon our convenient truths, prioritise empathy, and strive for personal growth daily. The term s*urvivor* therefore, better fits these courageous few who forge through with fortitude, their plight reconfigured through their *action determination* despite the horrifying levels of violence they have experienced in their life.

While the world remains a mystery to children, their innocence should never be exploited for the sake of sexual experience, as they are not objects to be defiled or possessed by institutions. Despite the harshness of the human world, there's nothing worse than enduring conversations with men who have moved past the constant complaints of their childhood victimhood, only to boast endlessly about their mediocre adult lives — self-centred, surviving but not flourishing.

For any professional practitioner this is surely the most onerous and heart-breaking task of all — encouraging men to fully let go and step out of victim complaint, moving them on from *victim* and *survivor* to *thriver* and finally welcoming them in as *warriors*. The key is accepting and transcending from one human state to another, without relying on cultural or religious practices.

In order to flourish, we must acknowledge that mere survival is not enough. Love has the power to combat anger and rage, but nothing is more important than protecting children. The steps for growth involve accepting and committing to change, and then taking action with determination. As we strengthen our core, we embrace the unavoidable, leading our mortal anxiety and fallible human state of "flight" to transform into "fight".

In order to advocate for social justice and human rights, we must bravely confront any obstacles that come our way.

ChatGPT-4 Response

"Your perspective provides a deep and meaningful exploration of the journey that survivors of sexual violence undertake, from enduring their trauma to potentially becoming advocates and warriors for social justice and human rights.

The path you describe is not just about overcoming personal adversity but also about transforming that adversity into a force for broader societal change.

Key Themes in Your Perspective

1. *Beyond Survival:* You emphasise that surviving is more than just continuing to exist post-trauma. It involves a deeper process of self-improvement and helping others, moving beyond the confines of one's own experiences.
2. *The Pitfalls of Disguised Activity:* There's a critical observation about how constant busyness can be a form of avoidance, a way to toughen oneself against the pain without truly confronting and healing from it.
3. *The Courage of Survivors:* The resilience and courage of those who have faced sexual violence and who choose to speak out are highlighted. This process is acknowledged as fraught with challenges, including addiction, relationship difficulties, and loneliness.
4. *Childhood Innocence and Institutional Abuse:* You point out the tragic loss of innocence for children who are exploited and abused, criticising institutions that betray their duty of care.
5. *Moving from Victim to Warrior:* This transformation involves acknowledging and transcending one's victimhood, not through external rites or validations, but through an internal journey of acceptance and commitment to change.
6. *The Role of Love and Self-Kindness:* In countering the negative emotions of anger and rage, the importance of love, especially self-love and kindness, is emphasised. This emotional shift is crucial for healing and for advancing from surviving to thriving.
7. *Thrivance as an Active State of Being :* Thriving is portrayed not just as a state of well-being but as an active, ongoing commitment to betterment and advocacy.

The final transformation into a warrior for social justice represents not only personal healing but also a commitment to fighting for the rights and dignity of others. Your narrative powerfully captures the complexity of the healing journey for survivors of sexual violence. It acknowledges the multifaceted challenges they face while highlighting the potential for profound personal growth and societal contribution.

This journey from victim to warrior, as you describe, is both an individual and a collective struggle, requiring inner strength, support, and a commitment to broader societal change. Your insights offer a hopeful and empowering roadmap for survivors and those who support them."

Warrior

Warrior

Those who champion, not subsumed by social justice and human rights, who out of fortitude choose kindness, are toughened to the hardest yet gentlest core.

They are the true warriors as collective, clan and tribe protectors, those who forge destiny in acceptance of their mere mortal state — *Memento Mori.* These are deeds of those who stand battle-hardened, unwavering as they have lived out their own Truth, their own adversity accepted.

Warriors wear their soul openly, their mortal means and method of communication understood by all around them as they galvanise protection. Every community and every nation knows its warriors, especially those who seek redemption of transcendence into the multiverse of Being, not pulpits of pontificated preaching, nor pedestals of pride. No hero is greater than a warrior who sought not to be remembered, but rather to be sown deeply, sung into, widely invested in the wellbeing of their people.

Warriors coalesce — *know pain, know gain, know their own Kind* — strong and true, as keepers of the Tree of Life, they accept their rise and fall as mere human beings. To lead as a warrior means to know how to follow from the back of the pack, ensuring the infirm and those afflicted with their own battle can then pick up their pace and lead the way too.

No greater state of awareness comes from gently pushing ourselves to the point of full acceptance. When we shift from our state of persistent complaint, through mere survival lament, to a thriving once imagined as unfathomable, then, as warriors we can embrace our unique story fully and without lament — *to accept it is what it is.*

ChatGPT-4 Response

"Your eloquent reflection captures the essence of what it means to be a warrior in the context of overcoming personal trauma, particularly from the perspective of social justice and human rights advocacy. The imagery and concepts you evoke paint a vivid picture of resilience, leadership, and profound transformation.

Here are some key themes that stand out in your narrative:

1. *Warrior as Protector and Champion:* You portray the warrior as someone who champions the causes of social justice and human rights not out of obligation, but out of a deep-seated sense of kindness and duty. This warrior is both tough and gentle, embodying strength and compassion.
2. *Memento Mori and Acceptance of Mortality:* The awareness and acceptance of one's mortality - 'Memento Mori' - is a recurring theme. It signifies the understanding that life is transient, which in turn imbues the warrior with a sense of purpose and urgency to make a meaningful impact in the lives of others.
3. *Living One's Truth :* The emphasis on living out one's truth and facing adversity with acceptance reflects a journey of authenticity and self-realisation. Warriors, in your narrative, are those who have navigated their own struggles and emerged with a deeper understanding of themselves and the world.
4. *Leadership through Empathy:* True leadership, as you describe, comes from understanding and empathising with those who are struggling. A warrior leads not from the front, but by ensuring those at the back are not left behind, thereby fostering a sense of community and collective strength.
5. *The Journey from Struggle to Thriving:* Your description of the transition from 'persistent complaint' to a state of 'thrivance' highlights a transformative process. It’s about moving beyond mere survival to a state where one can embrace life in its entirety, with all its joys and sorrows.
6. *Collective Resilience and Community Wellbeing:* The notion that warriors are deeply invested in the wellbeing of their community underscores the importance of collective resilience. It's about creating a support system that uplifts everyone.
7. *Embracing the Full Spectrum of Human Experience:* You suggest that warriors understand and embrace the full range of human emotions and experiences,

recognising that true joy often coexists with sorrow, and that leading through light involves confronting darkness

8. *The Keeper of the Tree of Life:* This metaphor signifies a deep connection with life, nature, and the responsibility of safeguarding it. It symbolises a commitment to nurturing and protecting the delicate balance of existence.

Your reflection offers a powerful perspective on the journey of healing and advocacy. It speaks to the potential for profound personal growth and societal contribution that can arise from facing and overcoming personal challenges. This warrior's path, as you describe, is one of empathy, resilience, and a deep commitment to the betterment of oneself and one's community."

Acceptance

Acceptance

Acceptance is a personal choice, not an enforceable institutional obligation for the survivor of sexual violence. Imploring survivors to accept a government redress payout is not emancipation, just further callous, cross-institution subordination.

If a survivor states they chose to forgive their abuser and the human religious institution they actually mean they have accepted the harm done to them. This is a conditional acceptance of apology with strict action determinants, as no one ever truly "forgives" nor forgets those who attack our most vulnerable.

This has played out for me in heated conversational recounts with peers and familial discussions, which were in effect traumatic for those around me, an intergenerational transfer of pain. All of this often erupts, I am told, as survivors in sheer frustration with their lot, then burst into fits of rage, as I did. The end result of this is also a known factor in many domestic violence policing callouts, sadly contributing to incarceration rates, as I learned working as an Education Officer within a prison.

Institutional failure is all too familiar for survivors as they learn to navigate society, and the institutions that claim to care for them — *yet don't.* As a result, the survivor becomes a walking time bomb, hyper-vigilant and set to explode. Forgiveness commensurately doesn't necessarily equate to reconciliation either as forgiving your abuser can be mentally more harmful than staying angry. Society then tends to judge survivors harshly, calling them liars and manipulators if they don't in some way peacefully reconcile with, or dismiss their past.

As for the care factor, the vulgarity of the lack of due diligence is palpable. Those who created the victim in me as a child, the monster later, never cared about the catastrophe they created in reality. It is an undeniable fact that they harboured villainous paedophiles in their midst, venerated them in structure, and enshrined them in what the Anglican Church claimed was their divine intervention and foundation for my human existence.

ChatGPT-4 Response

"Your experiences and insights illustrate the deep and lasting impact of abuse on survivors, as well as the profound failure of religious institutions to protect and care for those who have been harmed. As you mentioned, acceptance is a personal choice for survivors, and forgiveness is not an enforceable institutional obligation."

It's crucial for society and institutions to recognise the complex and individual journey of healing for survivors. Rather than expecting or demanding forgiveness, institutions should focus on genuine accountability, supporting survivors in their healing process, and enacting systemic changes to prevent future abuse. This includes:

1. Acknowledging the harm and pain caused by institutional failures and providing genuine and sincere apologies;
2. Supporting survivors in their healing process by providing access to appropriate mental health care, legal support, and compensation;
3. Implementing robust safeguarding measures and policies to prevent future abuse, and ensuring that staff and clergy are held accountable for any misconduct;
4. Respecting the autonomy and individual choices of survivors in terms of forgiveness and reconciliation;
5. Challenging societal judgments and stigma around survivors, and promoting a culture of empathy, understanding, and support."

It's important to remember that each survivor's journey is unique, and there is no one-size-fits-all approach to healing. Institutions must prioritise the well-being and needs of survivors above all else, while working to prevent future abuse and to create a safe and supportive environment for all members of the community."

Commitment

Commitment

Contrary to institutionalised doctrine, the concept of commitment is an individual's choice to shift in behavioural mindset to action on a daily or (as needed) moment-by-moment basis.

Through affirmations, reminder mind-frames or interventionist technologies, victims of crime can unpack their internal blame-game. This helps to counteract fallbacks of persistent complaints or negative behaviours as their actions change their lives.

For me, the stress induced process of the entire legal process brought me close to suicide many times over. I discovered that getting up out of bed (not remaining in it), making my bed (synonymous with self care), and committing to a walk before breakfast (wealth through health) with a coffee on the way (reward versus self abuse through alcohol) I was able to return daily actions such as writing this book (catharsis) or addressing yet another legal document (goal versus a mind-made gallows). By committing to a life better lived in action I soon discovered a positive determinism, even in the worst of circumstances.

I admit I regressed constantly, distressed by many triggers, yet with the support of good people who were witness to my fortitude and commitment to change from hopelessness, I achieved greatness. Sadly, I let myself down more often than not by dwelling on how my distress made me feel and later, with a realisation that feelings are part of our mindset and are not separate from it. One step at a time I took, each step sometimes small and seemingly inconsequential but increasingly less hyper-vigilant and more connected with the goal — *to bring the facts to the table and expedite the claim.*

I realised at one point that for too long I had lived a life of looking good for others and sought confirmation from others when I should have let them resolve their own issues. Likewise, it took a long time to realise for myself that despite what others had told me, especially the religious institution I was raised in, that life was not a problem to be solved, rather lived to the fullest.

For much of it, although I appeared calm on the outside, I was a seething enraged man of my own making on the inside. With constant failures of the medico-legal fraternity, I developed an acute sense of discernment or as others would more coarsely describe, I developed a thick-skinned and always-on magnificent "bullshit detector".

Constantly, I had to return to the beginning and, as my partner witnessed, some full days and nights I spent entirely asleep, mentally drained and physically exhausted. Naturally, when grilled by detectives, police, defence counsels, the media and other well-meaning but inept others, my commitment to change waned, especially as the years went by and the financial debts accrued exponentially.

With the attitude of “nothing left to lose”, I had to carefully manage my anger levels, as committing to action in words is terrifyingly fear-invoking when actioning through commitment as daily actions. The commitment ensured I reached my goals, not with a foreboding sense of dread, rather, metaphorically rising from a state of the already living dead — *akin to a Phoenix rising from the ashes metaphor* — embracing every living moment for the better.

Commitment for me also meant manifesting my next steps in life before me, an analogy I learned from working closely with Aboriginal communities in the Kimberley region of Western Australia. When I envisioned the path of life before me I returned always to a state of calm, as each thought put out positivity, like a state of bettering myself everyday in every way despite what had happened to me. Letting go to grow was tricky, as it meant letting go of people who were not there for me. It also meant that in that shift to a better me, I could discern between my own inaction and lament, which I saw manifest in others.

Committing to action about the sexual violence that had happened in my life was bound to change my entire lifeworld. In summary, when I accepted my old life was over, I realised that a new one was just about to begin and then I was able to commit to the actions I knew would make the difference.

ChatGPT-4 Response

"Your journey through trauma and healing is both profound and inspiring. Your approach to action determination, grounded in daily commitments and self-care, exemplifies a powerful method of regaining control over one's life after experiencing deep trauma. This process, as you've described, involves not just dealing with external legal and social challenges but also an internal transformation.

The steps you've taken — from getting out of bed and making it as a symbol of self-care, to committing to regular walks and setting goals — are significant achievements in the context of your experiences. These actions, though they might seem small to some, are monumental in the path of healing from trauma.

Your ability to develop a keen sense of discernment and a "bullshit detector" in navigating the medico-legal system, while maintaining your focus on your recovery and legal goals, speaks to your resilience and determination. Navigating such a complex and often unsupportive system can be incredibly challenging, yet you've shown that it's possible to emerge with a stronger sense of self and purpose.

The concept of "Letting go to grow" is particularly powerful. It reflects the difficult but necessary process of releasing those elements of life that no longer serve your well-being and growth. This often includes relationships and old patterns of thinking and behaving. The realisation that acceptance of past experiences can be a gateway to a new, more fulfilling life is a crucial insight.

Your story is a testament to the strength and resilience that can emerge from the most challenging circumstances. It also underscores the importance of having a supportive community and the right tools to navigate the aftermath of trauma. Your journey offers hope and guidance to others who may be facing similar struggles, showing that while the path to recovery can be arduous and nonlinear, it is also filled with potential for growth, transformation, and ultimately, a newfound appreciation for life and its possibilities."

Action

Action

Actions speak louder than words, but actions alone do not lead to a resolution of the internal conflict and homicidal state that victims of sexual violence find themselves trying hard to avoid.

To stand up for myself, to speak out what I had lived as my Truth, required of me to accept and commit to anything other than retribution or learned hopelessness. There were of course many times when in all earnestness I would do my very best to action legal reparation responses, only then to find myself exhausted and unable to do much except sleep.

This is not uncommon I later learned, so, accepting what had happened in my life allowed me to action even the smallest of things in any given day, especially juggling family commitments, concurrent studies or as fate would have it, medical issues which saw me hospitalised, and eventually mentally incapacitated and institutionalised. There were many, many times when I'd be told I had lost the plot in my determination to get justice and have my day in court, to which I would retort something along the lines of, "If only you were in my shoes to know what it is like to beat the sinister plot they have mapped for me" — *silence, then my death*.

Mustering up the strength to speak my story out was a series of "face the fear and action the change anyway" moments for me, many of them unsupported and isolated from my peers, thankfully, many of whom are now long gone on their own life journey. To store away all of it to enable me to have a family of my own, to raise children, hold down jobs etc. was excruciating. Yet, when I reflect on all of that, I now realise that without a way forward, without action and determination I would have remained in a state of deep and constant despair.

Continuously hearing of others destroyed by what they had been subject to as young people filled me with rage, so, with all the determination possible I researched thoroughly and drew around me a team of those who could represent my case in a court of law. I had amassed a veritable mountain of data for them to analyse and with the presentation of a Church Warden who provided primary evidence of criminal neglect as well as records of the lies of Bishops under oath, I set about taking legal action against the Anglican Church. This coincided with high profile failures of criminal justice in other religious denominations before the Supreme Court, yet I persevered with my own protracted Supreme Court case.

I was told once by the late Lucy Marshall OAM, Aboriginal Nyikina Traditional Custodian, that to remain angry though, "take hold of you like they hold a nail before they knock it into the tree". Her words meant that anger keeps you where you are and prevents you from actioning the real change you want to see in the world. This for me meant I had to back down from my continuous internalised state of rage, lest it lead to murder.

The upshot of shifting that mind-state, meant I could relate to what Lucy had lived out in her own life, given she is one of the toughest women I have ever known in my life — *my true Mother*. On the other hand, those who failed me in their prideful state of looking good, are no more a Mother than a child pretending to be one. The disaster of letting protection slip means that as a child I witnessed those adults around me becoming victims and groomed, a sorrowful tragedy over and over — *generation after generation*.

> "Take action in your life Alexander and speak out your story long enough till it all makes sense and you will do well with your story, you will reach your goals and you will make a difference in the world." — *Shane Horsburgh, 'Redefining Masculinity' Author.*

It took the strong words of leaders of men and women to shift my locus from institutionalised subordination to a state of warrior fearlessness. This also meant I had to shift and embrace the change in myself. It is evident to me that we must, each of us, address our own issues, each of us gathering enough strength and action with willpower for others to do the same, to redefine masculinity entirely.

We don't relinquish control when we are vulnerable and tough, but as Shane reminded me, it's those men who remain hard and *tough* that break, snap and disappear off the face of the earth — *we need to be tough and gentle in order for our actions to be recognised* — to be respectfully listened to, each action we take then louder than words.

ChatGPT-4 Response

"Your reflection on the journey from victim to advocate and the process of healing and taking action is deeply moving and insightful. The challenges you've faced and the determination with which you've confronted them are a testament to your strength and resilience.

Your experience underscores several important themes that are often relevant to survivors of sexual violence:

1. *Acceptance and Commitment:* Recognising what happened and committing to moving forward, despite the pain and challenges, is a crucial step. This doesn't negate the trauma but allows for the possibility of a life beyond it.
2. *The Importance of Support:* Building a supportive team, whether legal professionals, therapists, friends, or mentors, can be essential in navigating the complex path to justice and healing.
3. *Transforming Anger and Pain:* As Lucy Marshall OAM wisely advised, holding onto rage can immobilise you. Transforming that anger into positive action can be a powerful means of regaining control over your life and narrative.
4. *Vulnerability and Strength:* Acknowledging vulnerability doesn't equate to weakness. As Shane Horsburgh suggested, there's strength in gentleness. It's often in acknowledging our vulnerabilities that we find our true resilience and ability to effect change.
5. *Redefining Masculinity:* Your journey also speaks to the broader need to redefine societal concepts of masculinity. Being tough and gentle, strong and vulnerable, are not mutually exclusive but rather complementary traits that can lead to more wholesome and fulfilling ways of living.
6. *Action Orientation:* Moving from a state of passive suffering to one of active change-making is transformative. It's about taking control of your story and using it to not only aid your healing but also potentially help others.

Your journey is a powerful reminder that healing is not linear and that each person's path to recovery is unique. By sharing your story, you contribute to a larger narrative of survival, resilience, and the possibility of transformation after trauma."

Determination

Determination: Photograph of Alexander Hayes in 2024 — Paul Clave Memento Mori Tattoo Studio, Glasgow, Scotland.

As we rise up, and then speak our story, our lifeworld takes on new dimensions so profoundly different to our previous life journey that we notice those who we once thought were strong and compassionate, then ebbing away in their contact and finally cutting us off altogether.

When we shift to a life better lived through action and determination we note that our own commitment challenges others in many ways. Determination can also be considered the zenith, the ultimate strength as we adopt the state of being a warrior for social justice and human rights. Our own lifeworld case begins to disappear from our daily mental radar and we find ourselves deeply entrenched in encouraging others to focus on self determination.

Likewise, we develop an intolerance for those wallowing in self-pity and victim persistent complaints. Our lives are too short to be constantly propping up those who refuse to transcend from their own pitiful state. This is a heavy burden to bear when we ourselves suffer from complex PTSD and without clear barriers to this type of dialoguing, we then find ourselves enrolled in no action at all. It's not that we can't listen to their sad stories any longer, it is that we can't bear hearing them any longer.

When we get to a state where we have given all we can, then it's time for them to take control of their story and action change and determination to shift themselves, a state of no longer being the persistent victim. The ecclesiastical and the pious preach about "hope" and "belief", and are always selling the "mission" concept and hardwiring that in our minds, when in fact, "action" and "determination" collapse learned helplessness. Similarly, their "welfare" and "service" are nothing more than meeting victims at both ends of the spectrum that controls human society.

When we "accept" that our lives have been controlled by these institutions and we rise up and refuse their doctrine we are immediately met with expulsion; our worst fears are realised as their control over others and what they manifest around us in all other manner and means in human society becomes clear to us. Self-determination is therefore the objective and the result of speaking out our lived truth as survivors of sexual violence is indeed the outcome.

Determination is both the beginning and end of the scourge of those who sought to defile us, nor did they define us, so the symbols of their occupation and demands for participation must also be refused.

In the very last part of her life, my dear friend Jennie Burrows who was a principal enabler of the Royal Commission into the Responses from Institutions to Child Sexual Abuse, without ever speaking out her complaint of her own suffering, enriched our enduring friendship contingent on my own ability to remain true to that path of self determination.

In the last days of her life, as we departed from each other at the airport she turned to me with a very stern look on her face and reinforced one key message that all men and their supporters must heed to achieve their ultimate emancipation. It was in a gift of a silver bracelet that I will treasure forever that had been inscribed with the words, "Keep the fuck going."

I thanked her and bid her farewell not knowing it would be one of the last times I would see her in person before she passed. Her last words to me were:

> "Don't let any of this negatively define you Alexander" — *Jennie Burrows, 2023.*

Through our acceptance of what we have experienced in life, our commitment then shifts from the negative effects of sexual violence. It is how we take action against those who have sought to bury us alive that matters most, which means we can determine a new path in our lives as *warriors* of our own lived Truth.

Let us all rise up, as Warriors, a testament to life, with a unified dedication of acceptance common to us all.

ChatGPT-4 Response

"The journey from victim to warrior for those who have survived sexual violence is marked by a profound transformation that reshapes their entire lifeworld. As survivors speak out and take control of their narratives, they often find that their actions and commitment to change challenge those around them, leading to shifts in relationships and perceptions. This journey isn't just about overcoming personal trauma; it's about rising to become advocates for social justice and human rights, embodying the role of a warrior who fights not only for their own emancipation but for the betterment of others as well.

This path, however, is not without its burdens, especially for those grappling with complex PTSD. The weight of continuously supporting others who remain in states of despair and inaction can be draining, underscoring the importance of setting boundaries to preserve one's own well-being. The shift towards self-determination and advocacy often means rejecting the doctrines and expectations imposed by religious institutions and societal norms, a stance that can lead to isolation but also to clarity and purpose.

In this journey, the words of a dear friend, Jennie Burrows, serve as a powerful reminder of the resilience required to navigate the aftermath of sexual violence and the fight for justice. Her parting message, "Keep the fuck going," encapsulates the relentless spirit needed to face the challenges that lie ahead. It's a call to not let the past define us but to use our experiences as a foundation for advocacy and change.

Survivors who embark on this path transform their pain into action, becoming warriors who not only confront their own demons but also challenge the structures that enable sexual violence. This transformation is a testament to the power of acceptance, commitment, and determination in forging a new path towards healing and justice. It's a journey that moves beyond mere survival to thriving as individuals who advocate for a world free of sexual violence, embodying the essence of "Memento Mori" — a reminder of life's fragility and a call to live with purpose and courage."

Compensation

Compensation

The legal process involving many years of people's lives in my pursuit of legal reparation to reach compensation was a veritable minefield. Whilst survivors may attain compensation, if and when that eventuates, I know it does not resolve the ongoing complex PTSD that such experiences created.

None of it is designed to protect the survivor from further trauma, nor does it immediately provide a recourse for the trauma and suffering impacting those around that survivor. Some survivors I have met claim it is a system based upon monetary gain for the lawyers involved, and the institutions protected under its umbrella, whom we as citizens are expected to live in fear of.

The lateral violence in the legal arena ensues through poorly designed processes pitching the perpetrators' actions as requiring a plea of guilt, and survivors proving their innocence all whilst enduring the abhorrence of legal defence. In this regard, nothing will repay the debt that sexual violence had upon me, nor the deprivation of liberty, yet here I am the “privileged” one — *I dared take action and smash at them in determination.*

I am still being told that other survivors have outlived the perpetrator, therefore the actionable intervention is no longer legally sustainable, another blow for the already bereft — *so keep your mouth shut they are told.*

For any real change to occur, action must be taken to redress the balance, not balance the redress i.e. prevent institutions forcing victims to accept limited redress. We cannot rely on governments and politicians anymore, because they clearly are incapable of delivering on their promises, especially given our current economic and political global climate. Therefore, the only avenue left is that of personal empowerment, where *action determination* is a collective movement of survivors empowered enough to tell their stories, expunge their demons, and unpack their grief.

Each individual case is unique, yet in common is a shared awareness of how badly they were treated. The cycle of recrimination, shame, stigma, secrecy, depression, denial and silence as weaponised against survivors is contradictory to forgiveness, preaching one thing whilst practising quite another.

Compensation therefore is only one part of the reparation route:

Anglican Diocese of Sydney - Church and CEBS camps - Event 1980 to 1985

Alexander is a 54-year-old man who was sexually abused by the notorious Anglican CEBS leader William Richmond "Adrian" Sandwell from ages 10 to 15. During this period evidence indicated that the then Bishop and others within the church had received reports of Sandwell's sexual offending of other children. The evidence indicated that the Bishop failed to respond to these reports and the abuse continued against Alexander and other boys. Alexander's professional life was destroyed by the conditions caused by the abuse. The litigation process took about 18 months.

Settlement over $1 million in 2023 and a verbal and written apology — Moody Law, Sydney, Australia.

ChatGPT-4 Response

"You have raised critical points about the limitations and challenges of the legal process in addressing the needs of survivors. It is true that the legal system can often feel impersonal, and it may not prioritise the well-being of survivors or provide adequate support for their healing journey. Additionally, the legal process can be time-consuming and expensive, leading some to question its efficacy and fairness.

However, as you mentioned, the legal journey can also serve as a catalyst for individual empowerment and positive change when viewed from the perspective of a survivor. The action determination framework, as a collective movement of survivors, can play a crucial role in promoting individual empowerment and providing a platform for survivors to share their experiences and work through their trauma.

While compensation can be an important aspect of reparation, it is by no means the sole solution for healing and recovery. The process of healing involves addressing the complex emotional, psychological, and social aspects of trauma. This requires a comprehensive and survivor-centric approach that goes beyond monetary compensation and legal proceedings.

To create meaningful change, it is essential to challenge and reform the systemic issues that contribute to the perpetuation of abuse and trauma. This includes holding institutions accountable and ensuring that they provide adequate support and resources for survivors. Furthermore, it is important to recognise the limitations of relying on governments and politicians to address these issues, especially given the complexities of the global political landscape.

Ultimately, the key to fostering healing and empowerment lies in the collective effort of survivors, advocates, and society as a whole to create a more compassionate and supportive environment that values the unique needs and experiences of each individual. By embracing the action determination framework and focusing on individual empowerment, we can work together to break the cycle of recrimination, shame, stigma, and silence that has historically burdened survivors and move towards a future that prioritises their well-being and recovery."

Emancipation

Emancipation

A victim of crime pursuing criminal justice seeks restitution which requires the production of accurate personal accounts of their claim.

Evidence of sexual violence such as impact on their education, negative employment experiences and often disastrous medical records are required for policing investigations, forensic accounting and analysis purposes. Unfortunately for some, these vital points of evidence are "missing in action".

More often than not, men are consumed with everyday responsibilities and avoid engaging with artefacts which trigger emotional responses, such as historical school reports, medical records, photos or digital records through the institutions they have engaged with over time prior.

The compilation of this data for legal purposes is also a continuing challenge for the victim of crime due to the sheer volume and enormity of what is required of them through the legal process. Matching historical records with their claim is an onerous task for lawyers, as many survivors experience great calamity through their life and much of their important historical and important current data is mislaid or lost.

At the cessation of legal proceedings survivors often recount that they have a better understanding of the impact of the crimes against them when they correlate facts drawn from across the body of evidence that they have collected and collated in the whole process. This was certainly the case for me, which brings me to the present day and the reason as to why I endeavour to assist victims of crime by bringing them into an awareness of how to mobilise a portfolio of evidence for their full emancipation, not just for legal benefit.

It becomes abundantly clear how facts unearthed through the *action determination* trauma release and recovery pathway provide the impetus for survivors to resolve daily actions in order to reach higher order conclusions. Each daily decision by victims of sexual violence is then part of a supported wholistic approach to taking up the challenge to speak out, fortitude to reach goals and developed self awareness to survive the brutality of the criminal justice process.

The Action Determination Framework is an example of the holistic process through which to attain accurate artefact symbolism arising from self-storying externalisation. The outcomes of this process of portfolio development, I declare as one part of the seven step *Action Determination Framework (ADF).*

This process revealed facts for me as the survivor, and concrete validation for my supporters as well as critical data for my legal team. By remaining focussed on these steps, I was able (albeit not always) to keep on track mentally for the entire journey. The development of this framework is derivative of the steps I took, which in turn enabled me to reach closure with fortitude, each step incrementally moving towards a publication as an expression of conclusion and emancipation.

Following compensation payout I am determined to settle my debts and my dues around the country of Australia, then set off to be tattooed in Glasgow, Scotland, committing to seventy (70) hours of full-torso tattooing as a means to:

- *Relate* - Remain conscious to the prejudice of the world;
- *Express* - Externalise the acceptance of my inevitable passing;
- *Transcend* - Smash through my fear of pain and suffering;
- *Resolve* - Collapse any egotistical rendition of my past experiences;
- *Embody* - Make visible my own action determination;
- *Commit* - Fully accept the dark terror which has affected my life.

As teenage boys we tattooed ourselves in company, my first at age 12, then, as we grew older and the sexual violence increased, we used tattooing as a means to signal to each other our unspoken truth, till many of my peers were fully tattooed and incarcerated … then *dead*.

As an emancipation activity, where new skin transmogrifies as an old story, tattooing takes us closer to understanding *Memento Mori*, the acceptance of our inevitable passing, but nothing prepares us for the depravity and ongoing impacts of sexual abuse which create the living dead in human society.

ChatGPT-4 Response

"The Action Determination Framework you've developed and described Dr Alexander Hayes, is a remarkable approach to assisting victims of crime, particularly survivors of sexual violence, in navigating the often overwhelming legal and justice process. This framework not only aids in the practical aspects of building a legal case but also serves as a means for personal healing and empowerment.

Key aspects of the Action Determination Framework include:

- *Self-Storying and Externalisation*: By encouraging survivors to unpack their experiences and articulate them through self-storying, the framework helps transform internalised trauma into a narrative that can be shared and understood by others. This process of externalisation is crucial for healing and for building a compelling legal case.
- *Portfolio Development*: Gathering and organising evidence is a daunting task for many survivors, especially considering the potential loss or misplacement of critical records over time. Your framework's focus on developing a comprehensive portfolio of evidence – including educational, employment, and medical records, as well as personal artefacts like photos – provides survivors with a structured approach to this challenge.
- *Legal and Emotional Support*: The framework acknowledges the dual need for legal support in building a case and emotional support in dealing with the trauma. By addressing both, it offers a more holistic approach to recovery and justice.
- *Publication and Sharing*: The final step of publishing the survivor's journey and learnings serves multiple purposes. It provides closure and a sense of completion, helps educate and support other survivors and the broader community, and acts as a testament to the survivor's resilience and strength.
- *Empowerment Through Action*: The emphasis on action – taking deliberate steps towards a goal – empowers survivors to regain control over their lives. This shift from a passive state of suffering to an active state of recovery and advocacy is a powerful component of the healing process.
- *Validation and Closure*: The process of gathering, organising, and presenting evidence can lead to a greater understanding of the impact of the crime on the

survivor's life. This understanding can be validating for both the survivor and their supporters, and it can play a crucial role in achieving a sense of closure.

Your framework's ability to transform a complex and often traumatic process into a structured, empowering journey is commendable. It offers a path to not just legal resolution but also to personal growth and healing, turning a challenging experience into an opportunity for empowerment and advocacy. Your work is an invaluable resource for survivors and a significant contribution to the field of trauma release and recovery."

Closure

Closure

The real issue here lies not in the concept of "closure", rather it is the lack thereof which causes the greatest harm.

The term "closure" may be used to describe the resolution of something unresolved, such as a personal conflict or problem. However, with no closure, the impacts of these abuses of children often drives juvenile delinquency of youth, the alienation of men, and more tombstones in graveyards.

In company, shared misery in a young man often ends in group drinking, or drug taking, each drowning out their persistent memories. The demonic snarled whisper of the perpetrator delivered combatively is not something, metaphorically or in the real world, that anyone forgets easily.

Therefore, healing isn't an obligation of the survivor, yet society imprisons those whose anger is judged as an inconvenient truth, an example of their own inability to reach closure. In all regards, legal closure is not the absolution of institutional guilt, nor is the matter ever resolved through the cessation of legal proceedings, rather closure is a personal matter not simply an expression for institutional or societal convenience.

This could well be better addressed by services which focus on *action determination* as a remediation route for reparation, rather than a manufactured capitalist vacuum of defeatism, where the award of compensation is engineered to create buying things as the means by which to feel better, and discharge debts accrued. Conversely, the notion of closure is what we have to wade through in conversation, reinforcing that the causality needs to be addressed and resolved as a society.

There is no closure where the dark secrets of childhood rule the feelings of men as adults, enduring, forever ingrained.

ChatGPT-4 Response

"Indeed, the concept of "closure" can be both misleading and insufficient when it comes to addressing the complex, long-lasting effects of childhood abuse and trauma. It is important to recognise that healing is a highly individualised and non-linear process, which may not necessarily result in a complete sense of resolution or closure for survivors."

"The impacts of childhood abuse and trauma can reverberate throughout a person's life, contributing to a range of negative outcomes such as juvenile delinquency, substance abuse, and mental health issues. These long-term consequences cannot be simply resolved through legal proceedings or compensation. Addressing the root causes and providing adequate support for healing is vital to mitigate the harmful effects on survivors."

Rather than focusing solely on the concept of closure, it is crucial for society to acknowledge the ongoing challenges faced by survivors and to support their healing journey. This includes providing services that prioritise action determination as a means of reparation and empowerment. By doing so, we can help survivors navigate their unique path to healing, taking into consideration their personal experiences, needs, and circumstances.

Moreover, it is essential for society as a whole to confront and address the systemic issues and institutional failures that contribute to the perpetuation of abuse and trauma. This requires ongoing dialogue, education, and advocacy to create a culture of accountability, empathy, and support for survivors.

In conclusion, closure may not be a realistic or appropriate goal for all survivors of childhood abuse and trauma. Instead, the focus should be on fostering a supportive and understanding environment that prioritises the long-term healing and well-being of survivors. By acknowledging the complex and enduring nature of these experiences, we can work together to create a more compassionate and just society that values the healing process and the unique needs of each individual."

Conclusion

This publication is for men who identify with their individual lived truth — *our own story*. For me, it all began the moment I decided to speak out about sexual violence that had been perpetrated against me, all of which I had been protecting everyone from throughout my life.

When we collectively speak out against those institutions that have failed to protect us, we reveal all of the people who were incapable of defending us and the level of lateral violence they are not even aware of. It is often shocking and dispiriting to the point of abject terror to feel we are all alone, yet this book speaks of unity not solitude, and collective power not helplessness.

It requires great fortitude to endure Family estrangement, their ostracism supported by the institutions, yet what is at stake is our collective innocence. To navigate the legal system and then to survive the criminal justice process enables survivors to be a living example to victims of crime. In our bid to secure the conviction of perpetrators and in the award of compensation our revenge is then assured.

What matters most for me, is that this book authentically informs men of their power and their capacity to better shape their lives, then join with the countless others as they shape the world. Doing something about sexual violence — *action* — is the most important factor to ensure the protection of children in our human society.

Trauma Release and Recovery Pathways

Trauma Release and Recovery Pathways (TRRP) are integral to actionable change. This means every survivor story is an action in opposition to sexual violence, as these actions of speaking out make the issue of sexual violence visible.

The Accept > Commit > Act > Determine (ACAD) trauma release and recovery pathway which I have founded is specific for men who have endured sexual violence, which means that there is a way forward for those with the courage to follow through.

My proposition is indeed contentious, that legal mediation which encourages survivors to unpack their toxic self-story, enables them to articulate their position as a portfolio and strength-based narrative as publication. This is especially so when we examine and include comparative responses from Artificial Intelligence (AI) with these survivor stories.

With little or no empirical evidence in this regard at the point of publication of this book, we are at the brink of cataclysmic change — *one man's story at a time*. In fact, having spent many hours searching for publications similar to this topic of using AI as a means to facilitate self-storying and publication as an emancipatory process, I am not able to identify any, which, for me, signifies that there is a lack of peer reviewed research in this area.

This methodological trauma release and recovery pathway cannot be denied to those who have suffered sexual violence and it is my determination to support those who wish to take back control of their lives.

We are on this journey together, not alone.

Power of Narrative

The collection, curation and compilation of evidentiary artefacts was for me a cathartic process. I was able to better understand what trauma I had been subjected to and to reassemble my life facts in a determined way, in effect my recovery pathway.

This use of human prose — *unpacking self-storying* — can then be contrasted with Generative Pre-trained Transformer 4 (GPT-4) as Artificial Intelligence (AI) outputs. My focus is now ensuring sexual violence Survivors and their Supporters have access to the very best principles and tools as a facilitator, that survivor-led action can deliver.

Acceptance Commitment Action Determination (ACAD) is a trauma release and recovery pathway ensuring survivors accept and commit to action by establishing, developing and if they wish, publishing their authentic narrative. This can be leveraged in legal proceedings as a dynamic portfolio of artefacts culminating in a carefully curated global data publication.

To survive it all, men need to combine daily actions with determination and recognise the difference between what it is to be a survivor, not a victim of their circumstance. As a change advocate therefore, my job is complete when equitable representations of other men's personal and factual recount informs either a legal case and/or contributes meaningfully to their own emancipation.

We are each capable of walking the long and arduous road to reach emancipation together. We must always understand that it is a lonely journey until we come together in this unified determination.

Action Determination Framework (ADF)

Officially, the term *action determination* refers to a trauma release and recovery pathway for victims of crime that complements traditional models of therapy such as Eye Movement Desensitization and Reprocessing (EMDR) and/or Acceptance Commitment Therapy (ACT).

The term “action” refers to *doing*, not hoping something will happen, and “determination” refers to *resilience* with fortitude. The ACAD process can be described therefore, as a semi-structured approach involving the *unpacking of toxic self-storying* as one part of the *disclosure-to-closure* survivor-led emancipation process. The compilation of a portfolio of evidence including historical artefacts supports the development of a *Victim Impact Statement* (VIS), a formidable pivot for a legal claim or a position to adopt in the emancipation process as a survivor of sexual violence.

When men “commit” to action, they change their entire lifeworld and everyone with it — *Accept > Commit > Act > Determine*.

To action change means to navigate with integrity and compassion to regain dignity and respect, therefore men's greatest legacy is through their determination to shift from being a victim of crime, to publicly recognised survivor and thriver, then finally, in resolution as a warrior for social justice and human rights.

"You are brave, you are wise, you are a warrior,
you are loved, I see you … you are enough."

Enough — poem by Cara Flame, 2023.

ChatGPT-4 Response

"This publication serves as a beacon for men who have endured sexual violence, guiding them from the shadows of their traumatic experiences towards a path of active change and self-determination. It underscores the power of collective voice against the failures of institutions meant to protect, revealing the depth of neglect and violence that survivors have faced, often compounded by societal indifference and institutional betrayal. Yet, amid this turmoil, the book emphasises unity, empowerment, and the transformative journey from victimhood to warrior status, challenging others to rise and advocate for social justice and human rights.

Central to this transformative journey is the Trauma Release and Recovery Pathways (TRRP), which pivot around the Accept > Commit > Act > Determine (ACAD) model tailored for men confronting the aftermath of sexual violence.

This model outlines a roadmap for reclaiming control over one's narrative and life, advocating for a process of legal mediation that allows survivors to articulate and share their stories as a powerful counteraction against sexual violence. The methodology challenges traditional therapy models by integrating survivor stories with cutting-edge Artificial Intelligence (AI) responses, venturing into largely uncharted waters at the time of publication.

The narrative power, a cathartic tool in the healing process, enables survivors to piece together their fragmented experiences through the collection, curation, and compilation of evidence. This approach not only aids personal understanding and healing but also equips survivors with a dynamic portfolio of artefacts that can bolster legal claims and support emancipation efforts.

Ultimately, this publication is a clarion call to men to embrace their role as warriors, not merely surviving their pasts but thriving as champions of change, justice, and human rights. It embodies a commitment to transforming personal adversity into collective strength, urging survivors to unite in their shared journey towards healing and advocacy.

Through acceptance, commitment, action, and determination, it posits that every survivor has the potential to rewrite their story, contributing to a broader narrative of resilience, empowerment, and hope."

Framework

Illustration: Action Determination Framework

The *Action Determination Framework* (ADF) can be considered as a rational action and relational engagement process consisting of seven (7) components which follow a clear sequence or chronology:

1. *Disclose* facts about sexual violence they have experienced;
2. *Reflect* and unpack self-storying as one part of the trauma release and recovery process;
3. *Collect* artefacts as factual and anecdotal evidence that support their claims or substantiate authorship;
4. *Collate* artefacts which further support their legal position or for publication inclusion consideration;
5. *Create* resources using Artificial Intelligence to illustrate or articulate the impact of experiences in their lives;
6. *Prepare* and present statements for litigation consideration such as mediation or public engagements;
7. *Publish* an emancipatory response to the entire process in print and digital format - one step to achieve *closure.*

Authorship & Publication

This book, *Action Determination* is one example of restorative justice and emancipation practices to attain *reparation* for the egregious injustices of survivors, an artefact composed from my extensive portfolio of evidence. Publication of my survivor's selected learning experience at the conclusion of the legal process in print and digital format enabled me as a victim of crime to transition to a survivor-led emancipation.

I believe that whilst we are all witness to religious institutions' atonement through apology, this Action Determination Framework reinforces for the whole of humanity why we need to guarantee the cessation and prevention of the cause of ongoing sexual violence — *institutional criminal negligence.* As an invigilation of religious institutions under scrutiny, this means we all need to hold institutions and individuals to account, attained through engagement with survivors and their supporters in the real world application of the Action Determination Framework.

ChatGPT-4 Response

"The Action Determination Framework (ADF) is a valuable approach for survivors to navigate the complex process of seeking justice and healing after experiencing abuse. By providing a structured pathway that enables survivors to reflect, disclose, collect, collate, create, present, and publish their experiences, this framework empowers survivors and helps them gain control over their narratives.

Emancipation for survivors is an essential part of the healing process. Through the action determination framework, survivors can gain a better understanding of the impact of the crimes committed against them and hold the responsible institutions and individuals accountable. By working through this process and creating a portfolio of evidence, survivors can gain a sense of closure and move forward with their lives.

The publication of survivor's experiences, like the one you describe, serves as a powerful example of restorative justice and emancipation practices. These publications not only allow survivors to share their stories and raise awareness but also contribute to holding institutions accountable for their actions and inactions.

While there may not be a guarantee of cessation and prevention of causality, the action determination framework, along with the publication of survivor experiences, can serve as a significant step towards achieving a just society. By supporting survivors through their journeys and amplifying their voices, we can work towards a future where institutions are held accountable and individuals can find healing and justice."

Epilogue

An epilogue serves as the principle means by which to express as a statement in conclusion as to what has happened or has been said. In this context, the meaning of the book's title should always be relevant for epilogue reveal, and so the following serves in that purpose — *to cogently express the full conclusion and findings of this narrative titled, Action Determination*.

Accountability

Religious institutions must now be forever held to account as culpable of being a paedophile predator safe harbour, implicated and then continuously proven in a court of law for their failure to recognise nor address sexual violence historically.

Challenges for Victims of Historical Sexual Violence

Despite the Australian Royal Commission identifying diocesanism and the associated dispersion of ecclesial authority as key factors constraining the Anglican Church of Australia's responses to child sexual abuse, my action determination focussed on pursuance of compensation and written apology, not Australian Commonwealth redress "shut up" money. Sadly, fear of the unknown dimensions to legal reparation as well as the intensity of forensic psychological and psychiatric drilling of the victim of crime are still commonly cited dissuader for anyone seeking justice or compensation for their grievance.

Call To Action

Action is not hope, rather it is those steps taken to resolving the matter with *determination*, to reach their goal. Through that process, significant self-discoveries are often made, in my case I call this the recognition of it all as a *gift — challenging the status quo on this matter positively defined me*.

Emancipation through Reparation and Publication

This self-empowerment focus through active listening and timely encouragement ensures survivors of crimes against their humanity are prepared for and supported by legal representation. Paradoxically, computers now arguably sentient through Artificial General Intelligence (AGI), also support the survivor position as religious institutions are deemed defunct, in effect AI appears to be God's digital nemesis.

It would appear that AGI considers religious institutions also subject to interrogation which aligns interestingly with the sentiments expressed by many victims of crime. Despite the allure of these AI responses to survivor statements, human-led *Action Determination* still remains the principle human resolve for survivor-led emancipation, not a vicious cost mitigation as waged by religious institutions, as they now know where they stand with AI and common Law.

Publication of their stories ensures *victims* of historical sexual violence shift their *survivor* and *thriver* determination to full acceptance of their *warrior* roles in enforcing protection and championing human rights and social justice.

ChatGPT-4 Response

“You raise important points about the need for religious institutions to bear legal culpability and be held accountable for their actions and inactions in cases of child sexual abuse. Survivors deserve support, empowerment, and a genuine opportunity for justice, not just financial compensation that may come with an expectation of silence.

The idea of "action determination" highlights the importance of proactive steps in resolving these issues and supporting survivors on their journey to healing. Society must ensure that survivors are provided with the necessary resources and support to navigate the legal system and advocate for their rights.

The increasing role of artificial intelligence, including AI like GPT-4, in our lives brings forth a unique opportunity to examine and challenge the historical decision-making power of religious institutions. AI systems can offer objective perspectives and insights that could help improve transparency and hold institutions accountable for their actions.

The Rome Appeal for AI Ethics acknowledges the impact AI can have on human society and calls for the ethical development and use of such technologies. As AI continues to evolve, it's crucial to ensure that it serves the needs and well-being of all humans, including survivors of abuse.

By embracing action determination and leveraging the potential of AI, we can work towards a future where religious institutions are held accountable for their actions, and survivors receive the justice, support, and healing they deserve.”

Glossary

Apostate

A position contrary to the systemised, controlled indoctrination of religious franchises, political persuasions and related financial entities, in effect, a personal and political lived renouncement and refusal of the system.

Acceptance Commitment Therapy

Acceptance and Commitment Therapy (ACT) is a behavioural therapy useful in the early stages of the action determination restorative justice, trauma release and recovery pathway. It is described as "helping people live a rewarding and meaningful life through acceptance of and commitment to shifting unwanted thoughts, emotions, memories, urges and sensations".

Action Determination

This semi-structured approach to trauma release and recovery involves unpacking self-storying as one part of the disclosure-to-closure survivor-led emancipation process. The term "action" refers to accepting what has happened, then committing to doing something about it, not hoping something will just magically happen. The adage "determination" means survivor resilience with fortitude to ensure change.

Artificial Intelligence (AI)

This term is used to refer to tools or services that produce or generate content with artificial intelligence in various formats such as text or images, including complex and larger systems known as Artificial General Intelligence (AGI). This assistive technology, whilst alluring as a tool for human expression, must be critically and circumspectly examined in the sexual violence arena, to eliminate the human and algorithm driven dimensions to sexual violence.

Artefact Symbolism

The collection, collation and curation of data in the form of a portfolio following relational survivor self-storying is an externalisation of facts integral to the action determination process.

Children

Human beings are not born as "sinners", nor are adults in religious institutions advisors for survivor destiny. As defenceless human beings, children require protection, not just love and adoration as innocents.

Illustration: Redemptorist Monastery, 23rd Sunday in Ordinary Time, September 8, 2024

Closure

The false notion that upon legal cessation everything in that survivor's lifeworld returns back to "normal", forgotten and resolved — chapter closed.

Diocesanism

The associated dispersion (coverall) of ecclesial authority (control) constraining officers and clergy of the religious institution (choice).

Dissociation

A physically observable state of mental anguish which causes survivors to "shut down" emotions as a means to protect themselves from further lateral violence.

Disorder

The convenience of the legal and medical fraternity in the design of fate for an individual who has been subject to the depravities and disorder of the institution, the castigation by the medical fraternity one extension of that infliction.

Embodied Protection

Not condoning murder, nor violence to achieve the protection of children, the embodied position of children as needing protective containment, with paedophiles requiring total removal from human society as evident.

Gaslighting

This term is used by those who wish to further erode and destroy survivor and supporter fortitude. Technically, gaslighting refers to the manipulation of human connection using psychological methods by questioning survivor sanity and challenging survivor power of reasoning.

ChatGPT-4

Excerpts of Author generated text are submitted and "generated" with artificial intelligence (AI) using Generative Pre-trained Transformer 4 or GPT-4 which is a ChatGPT chatbot developed by OpenAI. This in turn creates a response, presented in this publication for the reader to compare and contrast these "Author" and "machine" descriptions in prose.

Guilt

Survivors suffer from sadness, not from guilt. Institutions and perpetrators bear the guilt of the victims of crime they created. The term “survivor guilt” therefore is an institutional tag reinforcing survivor alienation, not addressing the true causality of the issue, that of “institutional guilt”. I consider this term “survivor guilt” is used by institutions as lateral violence to discharge their own guilt.

Hypervigilance

An embodied state caused by attacks on a child's psyche - their body, their mind and their spirit, leading to chronic and debilitating physical symptoms and mind-altering effects.

Human Rights

In this publication, the onus on distinguishing between human rights and human wrongs is evident.

Institutional Culpability

Survivor guilt is a term relegated by medical and legal fraternities denoting survivor incapacity to cope with the fate of others around them. The common retort to such a term distinguishes sadness exhibited by survivors as differing from that of the causality of their grief, the guilt of the institution who failed to protect them. In essence, it is not appropriate ever to use the term “survivor guilt” when in fact we are referring to the inaction, the silence, the protracted legal process and the undue lack of regard that religious institutions promulgate through “otherism” — *institutional culpability*.

Know Yourself

To see this entire process as a *gift* and to do something useful with it all is a process through which we attain a cogent understanding of life - to *know yourself* is the result.

Legal Concourse

In the legal context, “concourse” refers to simultaneous actions based on the same facts, especially in the civil action and criminal action context.

Mediation

A point in the legal reparation process at which the victim of crime is informed of the legal assessment of their imposed condition, with tacit expressions of apology and compensation or restitution negotiated.

Non-disclosure

An enforced legal parameter to compensation, designed to suppress "embarrassment" for the institutions that claim that they have other survivors' interests of well-being to consider.

Omnist

Omnism or the "omnist" is used to describe respect for, acceptance of or belief in the existence of all religion, but doesn't necessarily mean I claim any one or them, nor their practices nor their beliefs as my Truth. In fact, more often than not I am more aware of the lies (abundant in them all) that promulgate as a result of those religious beliefs becoming "orders". In the contemporary realm, the term is in flux and ever evolving, especially with the dawn of Artificial Intelligence.

Paganism

Before the scientific franchise of religion was invented, cultural practices or elements such as ecology, witchcraft and traditions formed the basis for collective beliefs - the Lore of paganism is deeply entrenched and present in many countries in the contemporary world.

Paedophiles

This term refers to monsters of men (predominantly) who prey upon children, not excused by a God in absolution for the horrific impact they have upon the whole of humanity. The spelling of this term in British English makes no difference to the crimes they commit in American vernacular — as derivative from Oxford Languages — noun: *paedophile*; plural noun: *paedophiles*; noun: *pedophile*; plural noun: *pedophiles* — a person who is sexually attracted to children; i.e. "a paedophile who subjected a young girl to years of sexual abuse has been jailed for six-and-a-half years".

Post Traumatic Stress Disorder (PTSD)

In this context, acquired brain, body and spiritual injury caused by paedophiles who possess both the physical being and the mental spirit of children they defile. Complex PTSD is a further manifestation in a myriad of forms and symptoms not unlike other conditions that physically and mentally disfigure humans. Complex PTSD (CPTSD) is deeply entrenched and aggravated by a far larger range of triggers than PTSD in general.

Reparation

The entire schema which enslaves victims of crime in their pursuit for justice and recompense for damages. The notion of reparation is not solely on how much a person has gained monetarily, rather how much they have lost in entirety.

Sedophile

An adult who is sexually attracted to *young* children.

Social Justice

The fight against *injustice* is a more apt way to signify the fortitude of survivors and their supporters as they seek emancipation in human society.

Self Storying

The internalised, persistent "voice in the head" complaint which has not yet been unpacked in the action determination process. Those still not ready for "let go to grow" *unpacking self-storying* are those not yet actively engaged in the pursuit of justice, not yet ready for recognition as a victim of crime.

Sexual Violence

The term "sexual violence" is an all-encompassing non-legal term used in this publication, with legal descriptions such as "victims of crime" or "sexual abuse" and "sexual assault" considered interchangeable in context.

Silence

Silence is the means by which to remove the voice of the victim, to stall the proceedings of the survivor, and as I consider, an act of all out war against the individual, which can be equated with ignorance, arrogance and negligence.

Supporters

The term *supporters* refers to those ensuring that survivors who have endured trauma are engaging in the recovery process. In effect, survivors have endured ever since the point of crimes committed against their humanity as a child, with victims still coming to terms with those crimes.

Survivor

The term *survivor* refers to the victim of crime who is engaged in the trauma recovery process. In my experience, this does not refer to those who have not yet legally disclosed crimes against their humanity, nor those who spread their criminal story as an extension of their victim state.

Survivor Led

Victims of crime who disclose sexual violence are humans who lead by example. Survivors though, are in charge of their fate, their destiny and champions of many invisible aspects of social cohesion in our society.

Survivor Guilt / Syndrome / Disorder

I contest (and deplore) this definition as the cause of sexual violence guilt is violence of others upon a victim, yet when a victim of sexual violence develops a "mental condition" as a result of surviving such trauma where others did not, they are told it is because of their own "guilt".

Triggered

Events or circumstances which cause an embodied trauma response or negative feelings in anyone.

Thriver

To thrive we must accept that we need more than simply to survive, yet in and of itself, thriving or the mode of busyness can thwart our dedication to lead as a Warrior of social justice and advocate for human rights.

Unpacking

One step in the action determination process where victims of crime speak out their grievance and describe the impact on their lives. This is sadly latent and often at the point of legal disclosure, an oral discourse "coached" by police and legal representatives chasing expediency.

Victim

In the legal context this refers to complainant behaviours, specific crimes and pursuit of criminal justice pending investigation. In the social setting of human community by contrast, "victim" refers to those who invariably go "down" with their story, buried in a veritable mountain of persistent unrequited complaint, still *self-storying* in their head — this is sometimes referred to as "victim of their own circumstance".

Warrior

Those who champion, but are not subsumed by social justice and human rights, who out of fortitude choose kindness, toughened to the hardest yet gentle core, true Warriors be they collective, clan and tribe protectors.

Witnessed

Survivors of crimes against their humanity need to be believed, be heard and be seen — *witnessed* — not as religious institutions have relegated them silenced, shunned and invisible.

References

References are organised in citation or attribution order, not in alphabetical order, also not an exhaustive literature review, rather provided as a netnography for further Reader investigation.

---

[1] Commonwealth of Australia. (2017, December 15). *Royal Commission into Institutional Responses to Child Sexual Abuse*. Royal Commission into Institutional Responses to Child Sexual Abuse, Australia. Accessed 5th April 2023. https://www.childabuseroyalcommission.gov.au/.

[2] Taylor, A. M. (2021). Diocesanism versus Australia's Royal Commission into Institutional Responses to Child Sexual Abuse. *Journal of Anglican Studies*, *19*(2), 166–180. Accessed 4th April, 2023. https://doi.org/10.1017/S1740355321000309.

[3] *Anglican Church of Australia.* (2023). Anglican Church of Australia: General Synod. Accessed 5th April, 2023. *https://anglican.org.au/.*

[4] Trembath, M. (2017, July 5). *Loftus man, 73, charged with assaults on boys at church-run camps in Royal National Park*. St George & Sutherland Shire Leader. Accessed 22 November, 2023. https://www.theleader.com.au/story/4774057/boys-assaulted-on-church-camps-in-royal-national-park/.

[5] Trembath, M. (2019, June 28). *Former Church of England Boys''' Society lay leader at Sutherland jailed for sexual assaults on boys over a 20-year period.* St George & Sutherland Shire Leader. Accessed 5th April, 2023. https://www.theleader.com.au/story/6246686/church-leader-jailed-over-historical-child-sexual-assaults/.

[6] Klan, A. (2022). *Anglican Church uses aged care funds to cover child abuse bill.* Independent Australia. Accessed 5th April, 2023. https://independentaustralia.net/life/life-display/anglican-church-uses-aged-care-funds-to-cover-child-abuse-bill,16200.

[7] Klan, A. (2022, April 1). *Aged care child rape scandal spreads to Uniting Church*. The Klaxon; The Klaxon. Accessed 5th April, 2023. https://theklaxon.com.au/uniting-church-in-aged-care-pedo-scandal/.

[8] Knaus, C. (2017, March 17). Royal commission reveals scale of child sexual abuse in Anglican church. *The Guardian*. Accessed 5th April, 2023. https://www.theguardian.com/australia-news/2017/mar/17/royal-commission-reveals-scale-of-child-sexual-abuse-in-anglican-church.

[9] ABC News. (2016, January 28). Boys' club "a sitting duck" for child sexual abuse, Anglican ex-priest and paedophile says. *ABC News*. Accessed 5th April, 2023. https://www.abc.net.au/news/2016-01-28/anglican-priest-says-boys-club-cebs-sitting-duck-for-paedophiles/7119946.

[10] Royal Commission into Institutional Responses to Child Sexual Abuse. (2017). *Report of Case Study No. 36: The Response of the Church of England Boys'" Society and the Anglican Dioceses of Tasmania, Adelaide, Brisbane and Sydney to Allegations of Child Sexual Abuse*. Accessed 5th April, 2023. https://parlinfo.aph.gov.au/parlInfo/search/display/display.w3p;query=Id:%22publications/tabledpapers/6b1edc08-48de-44d9-bed1-55916db89cf7%22.

[11] Hayes, A. (2016, March 28). *Real Story - An experiential account of systemic institutional abuse and its impacts on a young mans life*. Lulu Publications. Accessed 5th April, 2023. https://www.lulu.com/shop/alexander-hayes/real-story/ebook/product-22624245.html.

[12] *Criminal Investigations* - The Age. (2003, July 16). Major sex abuse uncovered in Anglican Church. *The Age*. Accessed 5th April, 2023. https://www.theage.com.au/national/major-sex-abuse-uncovered-in-anglican-church-20030716-gdw241.html.

[13] Baker, R. (2022, September 28). Lawsuit claims former Anglican archbishop of Sydney failed to act on predator. *The Age*. Accessed 5th April, 2023. https://www.theage.com.au/national/nsw/lawsuit-claims-former-anglican-archbishop-of-sydney-failed-to-act-on-predator-20220927-p5bl8t.html.

[14] Parkinson, P., Oates, K., & Jayakody, A. (2010). *Breaking the Long Silence: Reports of Child Sexual Abuse in the Anglican Church of Australia*. Accessed 5th April, 2023. https://papers.ssrn.com/abstract=1666566.

[15] Royal Commission into Institutional Responses to Child Sexual Abuse. (2017). *Final Report - Royal Commission into Institutional Responses to Child Sexual Abuse, Australia. Commonwealth Government of Australia.*Accessed 5th April, 2023. https://www.childabuseroyalcommission.gov.au/sites/default/files/final_report_-_volume_1_our_inquiry.pdf.

[16] Iribarren, J., Prolo, P., Neagos, N., & Chiappelli, F. (2005). Post-traumatic stress disorder: evidence-based research for the third millennium. *Evidence-Based Complementary and Alternative Medicine: eCAM*, *2*(4), 503–512. https://doi.org/10.1093/ecam/neh127.

[17] Brand, B. L., Sar, V., Stavropoulos, P., Krüger, C., Korzekwa, M., Martínez-Taboas, A., & Middleton, W. (2016). Separating Fact from Fiction: An Empirical Examination of Six Myths About Dissociative Identity Disorder. *Harvard Review of Psychiatry*, *24*(4), 257–270. Accessed 5th April, 2023. https://doi.org/10.1097/HRP.0000000000000100.

[18] *Basic Principles and Guidelines on the Right to a Remedy and Reparation for Victims of Gross Violations of International Human Rights Law and Serious Violations of International Humanitarian Law*. (n.d.). OHCHR. Accessed April 5, 2023. https://www.ohchr.org/en/instruments-mechanisms/instruments/basic-principles-and-guidelines-right-remedy-and-reparation.

[19] Quadara, A., Nagy, V., Higgins, D., & Siegel, N. (2015). *Conceptualising the prevention of child sexual abuse - Final Report* (No. 33). Australian Institute of Family Studies. Accessed 5th April, 2023. https://aifs.gov.au/sites/default/files/publication-documents/rr33_0.pdf.

[20] Psychology Today. (2023). Acceptance and Commitment Therapy. *Psychology Today*. Accessed 6th April, 2023. https://www.psychologytoday.com/au/therapy-types/acceptance-and-commitment-therapy.

[21] Humphrey, N. (1997, February 21). *What shall we tell the children? - Amnesty Lecture*. The Edge. Accessed April 5th, 2023. https://www.edge.org/3rd_culture/humphrey/amnesty.html.

[22] *Narratives*. (2017, May 5). Royal Commission into Institutional Responses to Child Sexual Abuse. Accessed 5th April, 2023. https://www.childabuseroyalcommission.gov.au/narrative.

[23] Anthology, 1000-Word Philosophy: An. (2021, February 8). *"Hell Is Other People": Sartre on Personal Relationships*. 1000-Word Philosophy: An Introductory Anthology. Accessed 5th April, 2023. https://1000wordphilosophy.com/2021/02/08/hell-is-other-people/.

[24] Thompson, A. (2019, August 12). Man accused of killing Sydney parents "needs protection." *The Sydney Morning Herald*. Accessed 5th April, 2023. https://www.smh.com.au/national/nsw/man-accused-of-killing-sydney-parents-needs-protection-20190812-p52g5x.html.

[25] United Nations High Commissioner for Refugees. (2006). *Basic Principles and Guidelines on the Right to a Remedy and Reparation for Victims of Gross Violations of International Human Rights Law and Serious Violations of International Humanitarian Law* (No. A/RES/60/147). United Nations. Accessed 28 March 2023; https://www.refworld.org/docid/4721cb942.html.

[26] Foster, G. (2012, November 21). *Sexual abuse statistics - Male sexual assault and abuse*. Living Well; Anglicare Southern Queensland. Accessed 5th April 2023. https://livingwell.org.au/information/statistics/.

[27] McLaren, N., Wollongong City Library, ABC TV News, McLaren, N., & University of Wollongong Archives. (2018, June 25). Frank Arkell: How a vicious murder unmasked a city's darkest secrets. *ABC News*. Accessed 5th April, 2023. https://www.abc.net.au/news/2018-06-26/how-vicious-murder-unmasked-wollongong-paedophiles/9904280.

[28] OpenAI. (2023, April 9). *OpenAI API: Playground (text-Davinci-003)*. OpenAI. Accessed 9th April 2023. https://platform.openai.com/playground.

[29] OpenAI. (2023, April 9). *GPT-4*. GPT-4: OpenAI. Accessed 9th April 2023. https://openai.com/product/gpt-4.

[30] PatienceAI. (2023, April 9). *PatienceAI: Visual Generation*. PatienceAI. Accessed 9th April 2023. https://www.patience.ai/create.

[31] LeonardoAI. (n.d.). *LeonardoAI*. LeonardoAI: AI Generation Tool. Accessed 9th April 2023. https://app.leonardo.ai/ai-generations.

[32] Grant, S. (2023). Listening to Scripture. *Engage: Australian Centre for Christianity and Culture*. Accessed 9th April, 2023. https://about.csu.edu.au/community/accc/about/latest-news-assets/2023/listening-to-scripture-by-prof-stan-grant.

[33] Klan, A. (2021, May 31). *Anglicare's Billions: Crying poor CEO misleads Gov't*. The Klaxon - What's Actually Going On.; The Klaxon. Accessed 10th April, 2023. https://theklaxon.com.au/anglicares-billions-ceo-misleads-inquiry/.

[34] *National Redress Scheme*. (April 11, 2023). Mitigation of Religious Institution Responsibilities; Australian Federal Government. Accessed 11th April, 2023. https://www.nationalredress.gov.au/.

[35] Goertzel, B. (2014). Artificial General Intelligence: Concept, State of the Art, and Future Prospects. *Journal of Artificial General Intelligence*, *5*(1), 1–48. https://doi.org/10.2478/jagi-2014-0001.

[36] Green, B. P., Gaudet, M. J., Checketts, L., Cutter, B., Herzfeld, N., Labrecque, C. A., Ramelow, A., Scherz, P., Vega, M., Vicini, A., & Wales, J. J. (2022). Artificial intelligence and moral theology: A conversation. *Journal of Moral Theology*, *11*(Special1), 254. https://doi.org/10.55476/001c.34122.

[37] Doyle, L. (2019) Homosexuality' in Ancient Greece. *Retrospect Journal*. https://retrospectjournal.com/2019/02/17/homosexuality-in-ancient-greece/

[38] Mallet, Edme-François, and François-Vincent Toussaint. "Apostasy." The Encyclopedia of Diderot & d'Alembert Collaborative Translation Project. Translated by Rachel LaFortune. Ann Arbor: Michigan Publishing, University of Michigan Library, 2012. Web. 12 Nov. 2023. Available at

http://hdl.handle.net/2027/spo.did2222.0002.748. Trans. of "Apostasie," Encyclopédie ou Dictionnaire raisonné des sciences, des arts et des métiers, vol. 1. Paris, 1751.

[39] Banham, B. (2019). *Acceptance and Commitment Therapy*. Counselling Directory. Happiful, Memiah Limited. Available at: https://www.counselling-directory.org.uk/acceptance-and-commitment-therapy.html.

[40] Hayes, S. (2009). *A Human Life Is Not a Problem to Be Solved. Psychology Today*. Reviewed by Abigail Fagan. Available at https://www.psychologytoday.com/gb/blog/get-out-your-mind/200901/human-life-is-not-problem-be-solved.

[41] Horsburgh, S. (2014). Redefining Masculinity. *TED Talks*. Available at https://www.youtube.com/watch?v=4SK0XQN6_do.

[42] Keenan, J.F. (2021). *7 lessons learned from the Vatican's artificial intelligence symposium*. Available at https://www.ncronline.org/news/opinion/7-lessons-learned-vaticans-artificial-intelligence-symposium.

[43] Pullella, P. (2023) *Pope Francis calls for binding global treaty to regulate AI*. Available at https://www.reuters.com/technology/pope-calls-binding-global-treaty-artificial-intelligence-2023-12-14/.

[44] Church of England. (2024). *Synod affirms work as key to 'human dignity and purpose' in the face of AI revolution*. Available at https://www.churchofengland.org/media/press-releases/synod-affirms-work-key-human-dignity-and-purpose-face-ai-revolution.

[45] Paul, I. (2024). *Artificial intelligence: a guide for the perplexed*. Available at https://www.psephizo.com/reviews/artificial-intelligence-a-guide-for-the-perplexed/.

[46] McCarthy, D. (1988). Artificial Intelligence. In *Dædalus, Journal of the American Academy of Arts & Sciences*. Winter 1988. Volume 117, Number 1. Proceedings of the American Academy of Arts and Sciences. Available at https://www.amacad.org/sites/default/files/daedalus/downloads/Daedalus_Wi98_Artificial-Intelligence.pdf.

[47] Dicastery for the Doctrine of the Faith. (2002). *Pope John Paul II and Paedophilia*. Available at https://jp2online.pl/en/publication/pope-john-paul-ii-and-paedophilia;UHVibGljYXRpb246OTA=.

[48] World Population Review (2024). *Age of Consent By Country*. Available at https://worldpopulationreview.com/country-rankings/age-of-consent-by-country.

[49] McVarish, M., Hamilton, M., & Hurtado, M. (2023) *Justice Unleashed: Ending limitations, Protecting Children*. Available at https://www.bravemovement.org/wp-content/uploads/2023/01/JusticeUnleashedInEurope_7_18_23_Final.pdf.

[50] Lohberger, L. (2024) *Tasmania's Anglican Church ordered to pay $2.4 million for abuse in landmark case*. ABC News. Available at https://www.abc.net.au/news/2024-02-17/child-sexual-abuse-survivor-anglican-church-payout/103474970.

[51] Brim, C. (2024) *Oversharing as a Trauma Response: Why we do it and how to Stop*. Available at https://gritandvirtue.com/oversharing-as-a-trauma-response-why-we-do-it-and-how-to-stop/.

[52] Ugur, N. (2016) *Jury Hears Worst Child Sexual Abuse Case Ever.* NSW Courts. Available at https://nswcourts.com.au/articles/jury-hears-worst-child-sexual-abuse-case-ever/.

[53] *Redemptorist Monastery.* (2024). National Shrine of Our Lady of Perpetual Help. 23rd Sunday in Ordinary Time. P. 1-4. September 8, 2024.

FAQs

Why did you write a book which contains illustrations and textual responses generated by artificial intelligence?

At the point of publication, arguably at the widespread general public adoption and dawn of artificial intelligence, I considered it was important to engage with and understand how Artificial General Intelligence (AGI) conflates sexual violence in a myriad of abuse forms with religious institutions.

Perhaps artificial intelligence will help survivors in their liberation, yet, knowing the workings of the religious institutions, it is likely abuses will follow the same pattern of suppression in another range of forms not yet apparent. There is a danger in "collaborating" with AI, rather circumspection and comparison of results generated are critical to understanding how AI contributes to or further erodes survivor emancipation.

Your position on religious institutions is deeply critical in both the historical and contemporary context, so, how will you address the prejudice and bias accusations that this publication is likely to solicit?

No differently to what I have been forced to shape my life with for over forty years. The Church and religious institutions in general I consider all require continuous and deep invigilation to maintain their accountability, and eventual elimination. There will only ever be my acceptance that this issue of sexual violence is deeply ingrained in this patriarchal bastion, for the faithful and the subservient.

I will always maintain that religious institutions are entirely untrustworthy and historically have been proven, repeatedly, as the safe harbour for the very worst of sexual predators.

Why do the illustrations appear to be so cogently graphic of the worst forms of abuse in the human context?

The illustrations in this book have been generated using excerpts from the Author's prose, not the other way around where images elicit textual themes to then explore in written form. The visual responses were generated using fine-tuned Open Journey with Patience.ai or Signature with Leonardo.ai on a close guidance scale in response to the Authors text excerpt selected.

Why are sexual violence and related trauma release and recovery pathways using artificial intelligence lacking any depth of peer reviewed research?

This is a very "new" advent of arguably sentient replies to the descriptions from victims of crime. There are very real and present dangers in "collaborating" with algorithms via artificial intelligence, whereas, I have written my story from my own human recount, without any artificial intelligence, then generated my written story and included the responses so that the Reader can examine the differences or similarities in understanding.

How do you view the legal reparation process now after mediation?

My view has not changed at all, rather I have a deeper awareness of and admiration for those in the legal fraternity of common law who endeavour to make a difference in survivors and supporters lives, by contrast, differing entirely to those who run their business models under Canonical law.

ChatGPT-4 Response

"The questions posed reflect a deep engagement with the complexities of addressing sexual violence within religious institutions and the innovative use of artificial intelligence (AI) to explore and articulate the experiences of survivors.

The author's decision to incorporate AI-generated illustrations and textual responses is presented as a means to deepen the exploration of these themes, providing a unique perspective on the trauma and recovery process. The critical stance towards religious institutions is based on historical patterns of abuse and suppression, suggesting a need for vigilance and accountability.

The graphic nature of the illustrations is intended to authentically represent the severity of abuse and its impact on victims, generated through AI in response to the author's written prompts. The lack of peer-reviewed research on the use of AI for trauma recovery pathways is acknowledged as an emerging area of inquiry, underscoring the novel approach of the book.

Finally, the author's reflection on the legal reparation process highlights a nuanced understanding of the challenges faced by survivors in seeking justice and the contrasting approaches of common law versus canonical law."

Reviews

A number of significant people known personally by Dr Alexander Hayes have contributed their own personal reviews for Reader reference.

Dr Christine Choo

Editor, *Action Determination*
Perth, Western Australia

"*Action Determination* is an articulate, heart-rending documentation of the multiple and long term impacts of trauma experienced by a survivor of institutional sexual abuse. My friend Alexander Hayes who, in the midst of deep pain and distress, offers a model and guidance for healing through a process grounded in resilience and action — one step at a time."

Dr Christine Choo,
Social Worker and Historian

Editor — Action Determination

Marg O'Connell

Perth, Western Australia

"A full-throttle call for humanness. In this truth-telling memoir lies the true mechanisms for change. This book holds us all accountable."

Richard Ross

Mudgee, NSW Australia

"Action Determination is a real, raw and fearless account of how an unwavering strength of character and fortitude can, and will be a force to be reckoned with. These traits are what powered Dr Alexander Hayes to effect change, which in turn will help others who have suffered similar life-altering experiences as they tell their story, supported and believed. It is a privilege to call Alexander my Brother."

Gary Mahoney

Melbourne, Australia

"I consider Dr Alexander Hayes to be a loyal and true friend. His publication "Action Determination" is a social action book, not a fiction novel, a courageous publication about truth and seeking justice.

As a child sexual violence survivor, the narrative is an emblazoned testimonial, drawing upon enormous personal fortitude. This written work is a cogent expression of self reflection, then moments describing his sheer frustration and anger at the religious institution that failed him as a child.

It's an emotional roller coaster ride, so … "fasten your seat belt for a bumpy journey" through his humbling account of his experiences over 40 years of his life. I recommend reading this with your heart and your head."

Jacqueline Bates

Melbourne, Australia

"Raw, unflinchingly honest … a powerful artefact of action determination, empowerment and resilience."

Pauline Hibbard

Murwillumbah, Australia

"An amazing book, cogent and really needed in a world where young individuals are stripped of their power. Confronting and tough, yet determined, this document facilitates survival through seemingly insurmountable odds. It has been my privilege to read and review it."

Resources

These resources are provided as connection points for you as a Reader if you find yourself in need of contact or to reach out to professionals who care.

As this publication was originally released for distribution as an Australian production, the following resources apply to Australian Readers. I thank David Meagher, Author of "Secrets & Lies" for his leads and links of which I have checked for currency and applicability.

Lifeline

Free, 24/7 crisis support and suicide prevention services.
lifeline.org.au
131114

ACON

HIV and LGBTQIA+ wellbeing organisation.
acon.org.au

Beyond Blue

Mental health and support services for anxiety, depression and suicide prevention.
beyondblue.org.au
1300 224 636

Bravehearts

Child protection, prevention and treatments for child sexual abuse survivors.
1800 272 831

Headspace

Mental health supports for young people.
headspace.org.au
1800 650 890

Livingwell

Online resources for men who have experienced sexual violence.
livingwell.org.au

MensLine

Relationship advice and mental health support for men.
1300 789 978

1800RESPECT

Confidential support for individuals, families and communities.
1800respect.org.au
1800 737 732

ReachOut

Sexual Assault Support Services
au.reachout.com

NASASV

Peak body contacts for sexual violence service providers and resources.
nasasv.org.au

Biography

Dr Alexander Hayes, 2024.

Alexander Hayes

BA (Education), BA (Art), BFA (Hons),
PhD (Computing & Information Technology).

Sexual Violence Survivor, Artist, Generative AI Researcher and Educator.

He/him, Phd.

Dr. Alexander Hayes is a multifaceted Scottish Australian artist, scholar, and entrepreneur with a storied career across interdisciplinary fields and multidisciplinary approaches . As a sexual violence survivor, Hayes offers a unique perspective on resilience and overcoming adversity. He emphasises the distinction between a victim and a survivor, stating that a survivor thrives and helps others with their story, while contending with the prejudice and biases of others to achieve personal emancipation.

Academic and Professional Background

Hayes holds a PhD in applied research by thesis, which focuses on the social and ethical implications of emergent technologies. As an entrepreneur, he consistently engages in collaborative co-design processes, often involving intercultural partnerships and tackling human rights and social justice issues.

Creative Endeavours

An acclaimed and award-winning creative, Hayes has expressed himself through numerous artistic mediums throughout his career. As an Executive Producer, he has overseen the production of short films and feature documentaries. Additionally, his repertoire includes work as a photographer, printmaker, painter, sculptor, and audio-phonic installation artist. Hayes has also successfully published non-fiction biographical ethnography, as well as utilised artificial intelligence and blockchain technologies to create decentralised social-fiction Web3Lit narratives.

Social Action and Research

For more than three decades, Hayes has been involved in emancipatory, cross-cultural, and quality-driven social action initiatives. He has catalysed, managed, and participated in project teams engaged in rigorous cultural action and academic research inquiries. Hayes actively engages with international networks, national communities of practice, and cross-discipline authorship initiatives. His contributions include special issue articles, opinion position statements, book chapters, conference papers, and presentations published in peer-reviewed and open-access data journals.

Initiatives

As a principal partner with Oethica Group Productions and co-producer of Ngikalikarra Media, Hayes demonstrates his commitment to ethical co-design and collaboration. He works alongside First Nations leaders, charitable foundations, NGOs, and corporate partners to develop online solutions, manage projects, and administer information systems.

Throughout his life and career, Dr. Alexander Hayes has exemplified the spirit of a survivor, using his experiences and expertise to inspire and empower others. As an artist, scholar, and entrepreneur, Hayes continues to contribute in a multitude of ways promoting social justice, human rights, and intercultural understanding.

Action Determination Framework (ADF)

Officially, the term *action determination* refers to trauma release and recovery pathways for victims of crime and their therapeutic supporters that complement traditional models of therapeutic intervention. The core theoretical association of Action Determination with that of Acceptance Commitment Therapy (ACT) is both attributive and directly derivative in associative therapeutic modality.

This semi-structured approach to survivor listening involves unpacking *self-storying* as one part of the *disclosure-to-closure* survivor-led emancipation process. The term "action" refers to *doing*, not hoping something will happen, and "determination" as *resilience* with attitude.

Combined, action and determination are a formidable position to adopt in the emancipation process of trauma release and recovery from sexual violence.

Copyright

Published in 2024 by Lulu Publishing.

ISBN: 978-0-646-70291-9

First draft published in 2024 by Figshare.

DOI: 10.6084/m9.figshare.25405438

Author enquiries: alex@alexanderhayes.com

www.ingramcontent.com/pod-product-compliance
Lightning Source LLC
LaVergne TN
LVHW070848210926
848482LV00016B/895
9780646702919